Under the Williamsburg Bridge:

The Story of an American Family

by
Frank Bari
with
Mark C. Gribben

Order this book online at www.trafford.com
or email orders@trafford.com

Most Trafford titles are also available at major online book retailers.

Printed in Victoria, BC, Canada.

ISBN: 978-1-4269-1815-5 (soft)
ISBN: 978-1-4269-1816-2 (hard)

Library of Congress Control Number: 2009938783

*Our mission is to efficiently provide the world's finest, most comprehensive book publishing
service, enabling every author to experience success. To find out how to publish your book, your
way, and have it available worldwide, visit us online at www.trafford.com*

Trafford rev. 11/6/2009

www.trafford.com

North America & international
toll-free: 1 888 232 4444 (USA & Canada)
phone: 250 383 6864 ♦ fax: 812 355 4082

DEDICATION

In loving memory of "Me" (Zim) — Merrill's Marauder, member of the 5307th Composite Unit (Provisional); 1/475 Infantry, U.S. Army, China-Burma-India theater, World War II; U.S. Army Air Corps; U.S. Marine Corps, 71st Infantry - 42nd Division (Rainbow Division); New York National Guard.

ACKNOWLEGEMENTS

Sylvia; Don; Manny; Eric; John (Baby John) DeLutro of Cafe Palermo, Mulberry Street, NYC; Anthony (Tony West) DeLutro; all of the old-timers from President Street, Brooklyn, NYC; all of the old-timers from Midnight Rosie's, Brownsville, Brooklyn, NYC; Frank Costello; Anthony (Little Augie Pisano) Carfano; Joseph N. Gallo; Salvi and the boys from the 4th Ward, NYC; Dr. John Loscalzo, M.D.; Dr. Marvin Frogel, M.D.; Dr. Donald Palmeddessa, M.D.; Francisco Muniz; Connie Steers; Vietnam Veterans of America Chapter 82, Nassau County, NY; N.Y. Mobile Riverines Force Association; Petty Officer John Igo, U.S.C.G. (Ret); Chief Matthew Peterson, U.S.C.G. (Ret); Petty Officer William Stone, U.S.C.G. (Ret); Senior Chief Joseph Rondeau, U.S.C.G. (Ret); Chief Warrant Officer Paul Scotti, U.S.C.G. (Ret) - author and president of the U.S.C.G. Combat Veterans Association; Tony DeStefano, Pulitzer Prize winning writer, Jim McGranachan, Public Affairs, USCG and Vietnam Veteran; Michael, Joy, and George Sheinberg, attorneys at law; Ting Liang Chiu (Leon); all of the working girls from Flushing and Chinatown who made my legal career enjoyable and who comforted me through my PTSD episodes; to Quan Vu; Miss Young; Mink; Fred Janzen (the last to go); God bless Merrill's Marauders and all of the River Rats from Vietnam; U.S. Coast Guard Squadrons, U.S. Navy Task Force 115 (Operation Market Time); the Riverine Sailors; the 9th U.S. Army Division; Paulie (Four Fingers) Zampella; John Correri, Sr; The Manhattan, Brooklyn, and Queens Private Sanitation Association of years ago; Carlo Menotti; Sal Sicari; John (Little John) Huebela; William Boyle; Anthony (Numbers) Camera; Baps Cappuccio; Johnny Mucci; Carmine Mucci; Joe Coty Trucking; and Emma, Jake Trager's fiancee.

Introduction

A bit over a decade before this book was published, I had just published an article about the Purple Gang, a ruthless crew of killers and bootleggers who controlled Detroit during Prohibition, when I received a call from a fast-talking New York lawyer named Frank Bari who wanted to know if I had any information about his great-uncle, a Big Apple transplant to Detroit named Jake Trager. My research into the Purples had never turned up anything about a guy named Trager and I told Frank this.

It is not an understatement to say that call changed my life. My background was newspaper reporting and while I had covered criminal trials and worked the police beat, I was fairly ignorant about organized crime -- my article about the Purple Gang (my first as a freelancer which netted me $100) was my only foray into organized crime writing. At the time I knew more about the Partridge Family than I did about the Genovese Family. Frank fixed that in short order.

Little did I know that in a short period of time Frank would introduce me to men who would only sit down with me after they checked me for a wire, and that he would take me to places that most people don't even know exist. I'm the only one of my friends that has a picture of himself in a Chinese brothel (it was not open for business when we went), or who spent a couple hours chatting with a Korean madam who earned more in a month than I did in a year. Few people get to take a walk through the holding cells under 100 Centre Street during night court, and most of us who do never want to go back.

That is the world that Frank Bari thrives in, despite everything the world has thrown at him.

Frank Bari should be the first person to have a cell phone implanted in his head. He is the only person I've ever met who could fill up my entire voicemail-box, which he did on a regular basis, telling stories about old-time and current wiseguys with names like Chinatown, Sammy Meatballs, Pep, and Tough Tony. He appeared to me to be a walking, talking encyclopedia of organized crime. He knew who whacked whom, who was "with" whom, and who ran what. I spent hours on the phone with Frank and everyone I worked with knew who Frank was and what he was about.

Over time I stopped avoiding Frank's calls and started paying attention to what he was saying when he told his tales. There was no way that anyone could make up the stuff he did and keep it straight. I started seeing some of the names he mentioned in books and, more importantly, in New York newspapers, particularly The Daily News and Newsday. We began talking regularly and until my knowledge of the Mob increased I bluffed and "uh-huh'd" my way through conversations with Frank. It didn't matter that I was ignorant, Frank did all of the talking anyway.

Eventually he opened up to me about his family background and his personal connections with organized crime. Frank knew all of these arcane details about the Mob because he lived it. As he talks about in this book, his family was connected to the Syndicate from its inception in the early 20th Century. Today, Frank straddles the world of the mobsters who once sipped espresso and loansharked, but who now sit forgotten by everyone but their federal probation officers in their small apartments watching television, and the newest generation of gangsters who have arrived from Eastern Europe or the Orient and traffic in automatic weapons and stock schemes.

Talking with Frank is like peeling an onion. Just when you get one layer peeled away, you realize that there is another beneath it -- and another below that one. I've learned about Frankie 13, the wiseguy, Petty Officer Bari, the Coastie semper paratus, Frank Bari, Esq., the street lawyer, and Frank the father. Each one is as different from the others as you are from me. But Frank Bari is not a mosaic made of different pieces of tile, he's more like minestrone soup, a dish that is flavorful only because of the many spices that go into it.

Frank and I struggled over this book for many years. He wanted his story told and I wanted to tell it, but there were too many painful details that he had to come to terms with before he would go public. At first I fought with him about certain things that I thought needed to be told. There's a lot more to Frank's service in Vietnam that Americans should know. There's also the time he spent with a group of guys near the Brooklyn Navy Yard that he prefers to keep to himself. Most importantly, I argued, you can't tell the story of your father's life without once mentioning his name. But I never heard Frank refer to the man as anything other than "my father," and it wasn't until the man was dead that I learned that the name I knew him by was just one of a number of aliases he had.

Although this book is the saga of a unique American family that was witness to a strange chapter in American history, it really is the story of what made Frank Bari the man he is today.

But, like an onion, there are still many more layers to Frank Bari. Stay tuned, this story isn't done yet.

Mark Gribben
Columbus, Ohio
2009

CHAPTER 1

In the early decades of the 20th Century New York City's Lower East Side was slowly changing from the squalid nearly uninhabitable slum of the early immigrant age to a marginally less-foul area of poverty and run-down tenements overfilled with the cast-offs of the Old World. The streets were dirty, crowded, and filled with a dense miasma of smells as the cooking odors of the myriad cultures fused together with the stench of horses and chickens and humanity. This was the reality to which the immigrants who had been promised the American Dream awoke.

This was the world into which my father was born and this was the crucible that would forge him into the tough man he would become.

My father was born on the kitchen floor of a tenement on the Lower East Side on a muggy June afternoon. He was the third son of an immigrant family. There were no records made of my father's birth, which would work to his advantage in later years. He was given a name when he was born, but my father changed names like the rest of us change clothes. To him, names were troublesome. Anonymity was like armor. If no one knew your name then no one could pin something on you.

In the shadow of the Williamsburg Bridge boys grew up fast and they grew up mean. There were schools, of course, and truant officers, but there were so many kids to keep track of that if a troublemaker didn't show up for class, well, who cares? The real education for kids like my father came on the streets where they learned that in order to survive they had to be tough.

My father was a hellion from the beginning. He rarely attended school and eventually the principal contacted his mother and asked her to intervene. She began walking him to school, dropping him off at the front door. My father, however, would continue through the school only to escape through the back door in search of his friends.

When my father did attend, he served as the muscle for two older boys, Meyer Lansky and Charlie Luciano, who would direct him to beat up other kids and relieve them of their lunch money and other belongings. These older kids, along with their friends Benny Siegel, a.k.a. Bugsy Siegel, and Frank Costello, called my father "Our Boy."

My father met Lucky Luciano thanks to his younger brother who liked to gamble. Once, when my father and uncle were under the Williamsburg Bridge waiting for a ride from their father, four goons from nearby Cherry Street came by to collect a lost bet. Instead my father stood up to the toughs as three of them charged. The fourth, an older youth with a pock-marked face, stood by and watched.

My father threw three punches and knocked the kids out. The remaining kid approached my father, stuck out his hand, and said "you're with me now." That kid was Charlie Luciano.

He did not limit his toughness to the school yard and from an early age was frequently out on the streets shaking down street cart vendors and other immigrants. My father's younger brother told me of watching with fear and some embarrassment as my father would take "protection money" from the vendors using little more than an icy glare. He said that my father had a list of vendors and would check them off the list as they paid. If they were short, my uncle said, my father was not reluctant to use his natural ability as a street fighter to hand out a beating. In addition, he would take some goods from the cart before he toppled it over into the horse shit-filled streets.

Having made his weekly rounds, my father would saunter up Houston Street where he turned over the money and swag to a hulking giant with a perpetual scowl named Jacob "Gurrah" Shapiro. Gurrah, who earned his nickname because of the way he growled out commands, was the muscle for another man who would rise to fame as one of the founders of the national crime Syndicate — Lepke Buchalter. Lepke would have the dubious distinction of being the only Mob boss ever to go to the electric chair.

For my father toughness demanded respect and even as a youngster he was not afraid to stand up to men much older than himself when they failed to show him the *rispetto* he deserved. For example, my father always wore a Jimmy Cagney-style cap and once as a youngster he went to a barbershop with his father. My father was not tall, so he stood on a chair to hang the hat on the coat rack. The barber berated him for messing up the chair. My father glared at him and removed his hat and himself from the shop in silence.

In the middle of the night my father cut down the barber's red-and-white pole and lit it on fire in the middle of Rivington Street. The barber had messed with the wrong kid and knew it. From then on my father enjoyed free haircuts.

My father had two half-brothers, the oldest of whom was cut out of the same cloth as he was, sharing the same larcenous heart filled with get-rich schemes. While he was tough and unafraid of a fight, he didn't have the natural fighting ability as my father. Instead, my uncle used his younger brother's skill with his fists to make money. Under the Williamsburg Bridge my uncle arranged popular, but clandestine (and quite illegal) "Fight Nights" where my father would take on all comers. Older men from the neighborhood, most of them hoodlums, would bet on the outcome with my father and his brother splitting a percentage. My uncle told me that my father usually came out on top in these street brawls.

One fight that stuck out in my uncle's memory was the time that my father fought another street hood from nearby Clinton Street. The kid, named Snyder, was older and equally tough and the fight was particularly bloody. Snyder would go on to become a member of the Amberg mob from the Williamsburg section of Brooklyn.

In between rounds my father said to his brother, "His punches are hurting me." My uncle unsympathetically replied, "Get back in there; your punches are hurting him, too."

One of the men who watched my father fight was Red Levine, one of Murder, Inc.'s top killers. I had the privilege of meeting Red Levine at Vincent's Clam Bar in Little Italy. He loved eating squingille and calamari with hot sauce. I was there with my father and another wiseguy and the four of us enjoyed a small feast of seafood. Afterward my father ordered me to drive Red to the Park Sheraton hotel in midtown Manhattan. I didn't like going there because some friends of mine had taken care of a big job there once for Carlo Gambino and it made me a bit uncomfortable. But I was a good son and I followed orders. After all this was Red Levine, a friend of Meyer Lansky and Benny Siegel.

On the way there Red told me several funny stories of the early days — "You shoulda seen dem fights your old man had under the Williamsburg Bridge, dey were somethin' else!" Then he handed me a .38, "just in case."

"Now you can say you were a bodyguard for the Great Red Levine," he said.

Red was staying in a penthouse suite at the Sheraton and made a couple of calls when we got there. Soon a bunch of high-class hookers showed up. I had one wild time!

"Now you know how we were in the old days," Red said as I was leaving. "Now give me back my gun."

Through Gurrah my father met one of the most feared members of the Syndicate: Albert Anastasia, and they would develop a unique relationship that served my father well in the future.

As my father counted out the collection before Gurrah, the giant turned to Albert and praised my father.

"He knows what I want and he knows how to get it," Gurrah said.

Albert, a.k.a. "The Mad Hatter," was in charge of the Brooklyn docks for the Syndicate and knew a good thing when he saw it.

"Maybe I should use you on the docks," he told my father.

My father's boyhood did not always involve violence, although violence and street smarts shaped who he was. As he grew older my father would fondly recall the horse shit fights he and his friends had with kids from other blocks and how they loved to play pranks. One of their favorite pranks was to sit in the balcony of the famous Lowe's Delancy Street Theatre and urinate on the heads of the people sitting below them. More than once they interrupted one of Eddie Cantor's shows as they relieved themselves.

CHAPTER 2

There was one man in my father's life who had more of an influence on him than probably anyone else. His name was Jake Trager and he was my father's uncle — Jake was the brother of my grandmother.

Jake was a native New Yorker, but he was living and working in Detroit as the Syndicate's point man there. It shows how influential Jake was because most of the booze smuggled into the United States came through Detroit. Jake had come west shortly after Prohibition became law in 1919, making the United States, on the surface at least, a dry nation. Jake was a smart man and before Prohibition became the law of the land he had already made contacts in Michigan with people on both sides of the law who were interested in continuing to ensure that the Detroit workingman had access to booze.

Along with his brother, Willie, and friends Benny Glass and Louis "The Wop" Ricciardi, Jake founded the Saw Still Gang, which operated near Detroit's Eastern Market, supplying booze to private citizens, blind pigs, restaurants and other bootleggers in a wholesale market. Jake had quite a reputation among bootleggers in Detroit. He worked alongside the Oakland Sugar House Gang, arguably the city's most powerful gang in 1923, and the bloodthirsty and ruthless Purple Gang, which was in the early 20s emerging as a force to be reckoned with in the nation's underworld.

Prohibition had been very good to Jake and the rest of the Saw Still Gang. He had developed a national reputation and remained close to his East Coast friends, Charlie Luciano, Irving "Waxey" Gordon and Meyer Lansky.

Because of this friendship, Jake would visit the Big Apple on a regular basis for business meetings. He would return to the old Willett and Rivington neighborhood like a conquering war hero, driving into Little Italy in his Stevens-Duryea touring car, which marked him as a powerful man to the immigrant residents. In a time when a doctor could make $3,000 in a year, a Stevens-Duryea Model E like Jake Trager's cost an astounding $9,500. Jake trusted my father so much that when he parked the Stevens outside that pool hall, it was my father whom he asked to guard it. In the crowded dirty streets of Little Italy, the brass-and-leather car shone like a beacon, summoning every street punk like bees to honey. This seemingly innocent job, keeping the dirty immigrant hands off the car, was in fact rather dangerous. First, of course, were the punks who wanted to take a souvenir, but more importantly were the rival gangs who saw an opportunity to plant a bomb or set up a hit to take out Jake. My father knew this and took his job seriously.

Because of my father's loyalty and his fondness for the Stevens, Jake promised that he could have the car once he was old enough to drive.

One of the last times my father saw his Uncle Jake, the older man told him that he was going to visit an old friend, Al Capone. He handed my father a wad of money and told him, "this is for your new bicycle."

My father was thrilled and ran home to show his mother, who was less than impressed.

"Gangster money!" she shouted, hitting my father with a broom. "Gangster money!"

Several months later my father learned that his beloved uncle had been gunned down on a Detroit street. Jake had been betrayed by his own brother.

Jake trusted his brother Willie, but Willie had a weakness that Jake couldn't understand and for which Jake had recently lost patience. Willie liked to bet; he would place a wager on almost anything, which in and of itself wasn't so much of an issue. The problem was that Willie couldn't pick the winner in a two-horse match race, and he tended to bet money he didn't have. He spent his portion of the Saw Still profits faster than Jake could pass them out.

Jake had bailed out Willie more times than he cared remember and it was starting to take its toll on their relationship. Willie didn't seem to care that he was taking advantage of his brother. More than once Jake had told Willie he wasn't going to continue to cover his bets, and yet Willie would come back within days with another lame excuse. Now, the handbook operators weren't even bothering to go to Willie to collect. They were going straight to Jake.

With mounting debts, Willie Trager came up with a plan to sell out his brother. The plan meant that not only would Willie's debts get paid, he would walk away with a nice profit himself. So what if it meant that his brother had to die?

Willie arranged a meeting between Jake and one of his creditors. The brothers stood silently on the corner of Hastings and Wilkins street until a large Dodge pulled up. Curtains covered the back windows, and no one except Jake could see who was seated behind the driver.

As Jake and Willie approached the car, the rear passenger's side window was rolled down and the curtain pulled back slightly. Witnesses would tell police later that Jake and the passenger exchanged words in low voices – it did not appear the two men were arguing – before several shots exploded from the Dodge and Jake fell to the cold, wet cement, his head making a loud cracking sound as his lifeless body collapsed.

When my father discovered that his beloved uncle had been walked to his death by his own brother, he learned a lesson that he would never forget. As it is with most mob hits, the ones closest to you are the ones most likely to betray you.

Family was everything to my father and although Uncle Jake's death had to be revenged, he could not bring himself to harm Willie Trager. Benny Glass, who was also in on the plot, was not so lucky.

Soon after Jake Trager died, Benny suffered a fatal accident. It is no mere coincidence that Pep Strauss, one of Murder, Inc.'s most prolific hitmen, happened to be nearby.

Willie returned to New York a wealthy man. His home was lit by brilliant purple glass chandeliers and he used some of his new-found wealth to buy several city taxi medallions, which were never cheap. My family always wondered where this money came from, although we had a good idea.

The Trager family showed no shame in looting Jake's estate. His sister Clara took all of Jake's jewelry and the Stevens. Clara also "borrowed" diamond rings from her sister, which she never returned. When Clara died in 1959, she left a sham of a will. As a lawyer, I looked at the document with a fellow attorney and we agreed that it was illegal, null and void. However, when no one protested — if my father knew of Clara's death he did not tell us — the will was probated. There was no mention in it of the Stevens that had been promised to my father by its rightful owner, her sister's diamonds, Jake's jewelry, or even of her home on Bedford Avenue in Brooklyn. Her daughter-in-law, Doris, lied to the court when she said that Clara did not understand English. That's bullshit. I have evidence that Clara spoke and wrote perfect English. There is more, but I am not probating her will here.

CHAPTER 3

My father had an unusual way of showing affection for his family. For example, because he was shaking down the pushcart vendors in Little Italy, my grandmother, desperate to keep her son from pursuing a life of crime, would chain him to the stove in their tenement. She felt guilty doing this, but this was the only way she could keep her headstrong son in line. To assuage her guilt she hired a violin teacher who taught him to play. He studied the instrument for 15 years and was given an expensive violin by a cousin. After his cousin died, his daughter, Marilyn, asked my father for the violin back.

"It was only a loan," she said.

"Not true," said my father. "Ziggy gave me that as a present."

For some reason — perhaps to keep peace in his family — my father gave Marilyn the violin. He never heard from her again.

Toward the end of my father's life we had the chance to visit Jake's grave in Detroit. When we asked the groundskeeper where the grave was, he jumped in his truck and sped away. We could barely keep up with him. He stopped his truck near a row of neat graves and pointed toward the far end.

"Purple Gang," he yelled, and sped away.

After more than 70 harsh Michigan winters the tombstone was immaculate. There was a photo of Jake on the large stone ringed in 18 karat gold. We have no idea who is keeping the grave so tenderly cared for.

As my father continued to grow up he ended up being sent to a 600 Public School for juvenile delinquents. It was there that he met another youth who would become a lifelong friend, Johnny Spinoza. Johnny was the nephew of the Boss of the Fulton Fish Market, Joe "Socks" Lanza. Although Socks was actually a soldier in the Genovese family, working in a crew headed by a crazy capo named "Trigger" Mike Coppola of East Harlem, he had the influence of a Boss.

Socks exacted a penny tax for each fish that came through the market. The tax was "optional," but the vendors who opted not to pay found it difficult if not impossible to get the union boys to unload their stock, which would eventually go bad. In addition to the fish tax, Socks controlled other rackets like loansharking, extortion, and gambling. Nothing moved in the Fish Market without Socks getting his cut. Johnny Spinoza and my father served as some of Socks' muscle in making sure everyone paid up. It was when he was working for Socks that my father received his first gun.

"Kid," Socks told my father, "You're good with your fists, but here is the equalizer."

Along with Johnny Spinoza, my father became involved with Albert Anastasia and the men of Murder, Inc. Spinoza and my father used to hang out at the foot of the Williamsburg Bridge in a candy store with killers like Bugsy Goldstein, Abe Reles, and a man named Harry Strauss who went by the nicknames Pittsburgh Phil and Pep.

My father was a self-made man who didn't rely on family ties to advance his career. He could have easily used the influence of my grandfather, Anthony Carfano, a.k.a. Augie Pisano, to smooth his way. Instead my father preferred to plow his own row.

Albert Anastasia took a liking to my father, but wondered why he wasn't working with my grandfather.

"I'm with me," my father said bravely.

Albert laughed and said, "No, now you're with me, but I have to speak with your father out of respect."

My father's special friendship with Albert Anastasia and his brother, Tough Tony Anastasio, as well as his relationship with my grandfather, put him in a unique position. Much younger than Albert and lower in the hierarchy of the Mangano family, my father had access to leaders in the Mob that others could only dream of. It didn't hurt his standing when Albert took over the Mangano family by whacking Phil and Anthony Mangano.

CHAPTER 4

Another man that my father had special access to is one of the most misunderstood and underrated mobsters of the early days of the Syndicate — Dutch Schultz.

Dutch was the undisputed beer baron of New York who grew up in the Bronx. He was born Arthur Fleigenheimer, but earned the moniker Dutch because he resembled an old neighborhood brawler. He never liked the nickname and instructed my father to call him Arthur.

The Dutchman had a huge warehouse in the Bronx where he manufactured a fairly good beer. Dutch liked to use youngsters as lookouts and he especially trusted my father because of my grandfather and my father's relationship with Lucky. This gave my father entree into the Dutchman's private domain and crew, where he met men like Abe Landau, Lulu Rosenkrantz, Dixie Davis, a corrupt lawyer, a stone-cold killer named Bo Weinberg, and a mathematical genius named Abbadabba Berman (after a popular candy bar of the era). Another member of the gang for a while was Vincent "Mad Dog" Coll, whose assassination my father had intimate knowledge of.

Once again, Coll's death was one set up by a man he considered a friend. Coll, who earned his nickname by shooting up a city block and killing a little baby, had started a war with Dutch's gang by going out on his own and producing beer. Dutch received the OK to whack Coll and went to Owney Madden, an Irishman like Coll, to set him up. Madden told Coll that he would back him against "that Jew" Schultz and the men set up a meeting. Coll was told to wait in a Manhattan hotel for Madden, and he was sitting at a soda fountain in the hotel pharmacy. Owney called the pharmacy and got Coll into the phone booth, away from his bodyguard. As Owney kept Coll on the phone, a shooter entered the drug store and emptied his pistol into Mad Dog.

His help with the Coll rub-out only made my father closer to Dutch, who used him and Johnny Spinoza for other special jobs. Whenever someone else tried to get a speakeasy to buy their beer, my father and Johnny were dispatched to set things right.

My father told me that Dutch was smart and always had an eye out for new rackets. He established the Restaurant Association of New York, which collected membership dues from restaurants around the city. The Dutchman was even collecting a tax from the coat check and cigarette concessions! The Association also dictated who the restaurants bought linens from and other supplies.

Recruiting new members was the job of my father and Spinoza. Normally the recruitment was smooth, but occasionally more muscle was involved. Violence wasn't necessary because all they had to do with recalcitrant managers was to show up during the busiest hours and toss a couple of stink bombs around the joint. The restaurant owners usually got the message.

Another of the Dutchman's successes was muscling in on the numbers racket, which had previously been left up to the control of the Black underworld. My father was there when Dutch laid out his plan to take over the Harlem numbers from Bumpy Johnson. Joey Rao, Vito Genovese, Frank Costello, Lucky, and others were present.

Most of the men laughed because the racket was a penny ante game to them. When Abbadabba Berman laid out the math, the men stopped laughing. The take, according to Berman, was a million dollars each month. Dutch got the go-ahead to move in on Johnson.

How and why Dutch Schultz was whacked has always been inaccurately told. I know this because I was told the true story by the man who carried out the hit, Charlie "The Bug" Workman, a premier hitman for Murder, Inc. Charlie served 20 years in a Jersey prison for killing the Dutchman.

I had the pleasure of meeting and getting to know Charlie upon his release from prison. Two decades behind bars didn't change the Bug much. When I met him, he and another man from the Genovese family had recently seized control of the stagehands union and several supermarket unions.

Charlie told me the real reason that Dutch Schultz was killed, and he was adamant that Dutch's threat to kill special prosecutor Thomas Dewey was not the main reason Dutch had to die.

The story goes that Dutch viewed Dewey as a guy who had it in for him and that he wanted to take out the prosecutor first. The rest of the Syndicate leaders thought this was a bad idea because killing a prosecutor would bring down all kinds of heat.

While Dutch did want to take care of Dewey once and for all, it was, Charlie told me, Dutch's move to New Jersey that brought about his death.

Through the brilliant mechanization of Dixie Davis the lawyer, Dutch had recently beaten a case upstate that should have been a slam-dunk for the prosecution and was feeling nearly invulnerable. He was concerned about Dewey's investigation into his rackets and was not afraid to ask for a hit on the prosecutor, but generally Dutch was feeling really good about things when he returned to New York City.

He did have some unfinished business, however. It seems that while Dutch was upstate fighting his murder rap, Lucky Luciano was moving in on his rackets in the city. It was nothing personal, only business — no one expected Dutch to beat the charges. Lucky was working on Dutch's top lieutenant, Bo Weinberg, trying to get him to switch loyalties. Lucky won over Bo, who gave away everything Dutch had built. For his disloyalty Bo Weinberg was dropped into the East River, his feet encased in a pail filled with concrete — giving birth to the term "cement overshoes."

Having dispensed with his disloyal lieutenant, Dutch turned to his fellow mobsters who had been drooling over his rackets, but they simply shrugged, unwilling to relinquish what Bo had surrendered.

Left with nothing, but still feeling invulnerable, Dutch Schultz decided to start over in Newark, New Jersey. Unfortunately, New Jersey was already taken by Longy Zwillman who operated under the authority of Lucky and the rest of the Syndicate leaders. According to Charlie Workman — and confirmed by another very reputable source whom I wish to keep anonymous — Longy brought his beef to the New York bosses and they voted to hit the Dutchman. He might have been a brilliant racketeer and tough guy, but there was no room left for Dutch Schultz.

Benny Siegel, who at the time was still in charge of the Bugs and Meyer mob, insisted that he be allowed to participate, reminding the Syndicate board that an old rule (now abandoned for obvious reasons) required that a Boss be at the scene of another Boss's hit. The question remained about who else would be part of the murder crew. The bosses agreed that the shooters all had to be Jewish, because Dutch would be wary of any Italians who came into his place of business. That's how Charlie "The Bug" Workman got the job of rubbing out another of my father's close friends.

The Syndicate did not wait once a decision was made. Shortly after the bosses agreed to eliminate Dutch, a phone rang in the back of a candy store in the tough Brownsville section of Brooklyn. The store was known as Midnight Rosie's because it was open 24 hours a day. Rosie answered the phone and summoned one of the tough guys hanging out in the back of the store. Abe Reles, who would later turn rat and bring down his friends in Murder, Inc. took the phone from Rosie and spoke with his boss, Lepke Buchalter, who told him that he was coming over for a sit down.

"Keep a booth open for just us two," Lepke said. "I'm on my way down."

When Lepke used the phrase "just us two," Kid Twist Reles knew that something big was going to happen. He kicked out the lower-echelon flunkies playing cards but allowed his most trusted lieutenants, Bugsy Goldstein and Pep Strauss to stay. What Lepke could say to

Reles he could say to Bugsy and Pep. They were that close — at least until Reles sold out his lifelong friends to save his own neck.

As Rosie took the unusual step of closing her shop, in walked Lepke Buchalter, Ben Siegel, and Albert Anastasia, decked out, as usual in an expensive white felt fedora. Just a glance at them told Reles that this was as serious as it gets. No one had to tell him that screwing this up — whatever it was — was not an option.

The group huddled over a table as Lepke explained the situation. The Murder, Inc. killers each saw this as a once-in-a-lifetime hit, one for the books. Reles and Pep Strauss were eager to take on this major assignment. It was the kind of job that killers like them dreamed about.

"This can't be fucked up," Lepke said. "Sorry, Pep. This job ain't for you. Same to you, Abe. You will never get near the Dutchman with your icepicks and rope gags."

Although they were disappointed, Kid Twist and Pep knew who to use.

"The Bug," Reles said. "He's a good shot and he practices all the time with Albert upstate."

"Here's how it goes," Lepke said. "I want to use two cars. I need that big psycho you have, Mendy Weiss, to blast with his shotgun. He's a big motherfucker and who knows who's watching Schultz.

"Longy tells us he's there at the Chop House every night with his boys," Lepke went on. "If we do this right we can take down all of his key guys. While Mendy takes care of them, Charlie can concentrate on Schultz. Get a driver for Mendy and Charlie, but tell them to separate after the hit. Charlie gets in one car and Weiss in the other car we'll have.

"If Schultz isn't killed we're at war," he finished up. "We do this quick. Understand?"

My father and grandfather knew that time was running out for the Dutchman, but they also knew that it was time for him to go. Business was business, after all. They kept their mouths shut as Dutch's number came up.

Charlie told me that there was a musty smell in the air the night they went to kill the Dutchman. He described that musty smell as "evil."

The commonly repeated details of the hit on Dutch Schultz are as inaccurate as the reason why Dutch had to die, Charlie told me.

This is the story of how Dutch Schultz and his top men were hit, as Charlie "The Bug" Workman told it to me:

"Mendy was the first one into the Chop House bar," Charlie said. "He was wearing a black raincoat with a sawed off 12-gauge underneath. Mendy always liked them big-bore guns. Said nothing matched 'em for stopping power."

"I came in about a step behind him. I was carrying my favorite .45 Colt Flattop. It's a six-shooter, but I was cocky in them days and didn't think I needed more. Besides, I knew Mendy's piece wasn't just loaded with birdshot.

"He looked around and saw a couple of guys sitting at a table near the bar. I think he must have opened his coat a bit to show his gun because those guys blew past me outta the bar quicker than anything.

"Mendy nodded to the bartender, one of Longy Zwillman's men, who quickly hit the floor. That was one of the things that really pissed off Longy — that Newark Chop House had been one of his hangouts before the Dutchman moved in. The guy behind the bar hit the ground real fast.

"Because we had both been there when Longy ran the place, we knew that Dutch and his guys would be in the back. There was this short hallway that was about wide enough for two guys to pass if they're facing each other. At the end of that hallway is the crapper."

As he was telling me this story — probably the most important thing that ever happened to him in his life, something he had 20 years in stir to think about, Charlie got a real serious look on his already stern face and became almost angry.

"Now here is where everybody gets the story wrong," he said, his voice thundering. "They say I stopped off in the toilet and saw some guy taking a leak there, but didn't recognize him as the Dutchman.

"That's Bullshit!" he yelled, as if his feelings were hurt that anyone would think a pro like him would not recognize a Boss and a primary target. "I knew where the guys were and where I had to go. I didn't even have time to think about a goddamn bathroom!

"Sure enough, Abbadabba Berman, Abe Landau, and Lulu Rosencrantz were sitting at a table facing the hallway. I guess they figured that they were safe as long as they didn't have their back to the doorway.

"Well, Mendy proved them wrong. Quick as lightening he brought the shotgun up to his hip and let Lulu have it. I remember the buckshot hit him right in the chest and stomach. Guts went everywhere. He fired again and this time Abbadabba got it in the head. I remember thinking that it was funny that a guy with so much brains should buy it by getting them splattered all over the wall.

"That happened in slow motion like, but it really happened like this." At that Charlie snapped his big fingers twice.

"I had my Colt drawn and gave Abe Landau a couple in the gut," Charlie went on. "I felt a bit bad about that because I knew Abe and a gut shot is not a nice way to go out. But I didn't have time to think about it.

"Now, like I said, everyone thinks Dutch was taking a piss when he was hit. That's bullshit, too. He was in the same room with his boys, except he wasn't sitting at the table. He was off to the side..." Charlie pointed to a spot in the room where we were drinking as if the ghost of Dutch Schultz was standing there.

"He was off to the side," the Bug repeated, "enough so he could get past me and get into that small hallway. Now HERE," he emphasized the word, "is where the crapper comes in."

I was amazed listening to this man who had played such a huge role in the history of my family and my friends — and in the history of organized crime in America — relive that moment. It would be like listening to the Wright Brothers tell what it was like to take their first flights at Kitty Hawk.

"Dutch zigged around me like a running back and made a dash to the bathroom. I figured he was going for a chopper stored in there. Dutch liked Tommy guns and knew how to use 'em. "I got a bead on him and tapped off a couple of rounds and the force of the slugs turned him around," Charlie said. "But the Dutchman still had some heart in him and I emptied the Colt into him as he crawled toward the bathroom. I figured four shots with a .45 would kill just about anybody right away, but this time I was wrong. Dutch looked up at me as he laid on the floor. I swear he was grinning up at me. We both knew he was dying. If I had known it would take him a day to die and that he would go out jibber-jabbering like a crazy man, I'd have reloaded and given him one in the head.

"Still, I didn't feel as bad about Dutch as I did about Abe, because me and Abe was friends once.

"Anyway, I looked inside the toilet and sure enough, there were two Tommy Guns propped up against the wall. If Dutch had been a step or two faster, Mendy and me would have been as dead as Lulu, Abbadabba, and Abe."

Charlie stopped telling his story and looked me in the eye. It was like he was coming out of a dream.

"Another thing that really pisses me off is that people think I went through Dutch's pockets while he was dyin'. That's bullshit, too," Charlie shook his head and looked hurt. I knew what he was feeling. He was a professional and it was an insult to think that a professional like him would stoop to rifling the pockets of a dying man. He didn't need whatever spare change the Dutchman might have had on him.

"I was on a hit," he said. "The sirens were blasting and I never steal money from a job. All the time I was thinking about who was driving the crash car...you know, my getaway car.

"I lost sight of Mendy, but that was OK — it was how Lepke planned it," Charlie said. "I've heard the bullshit stories about how Mendy got pissed because I was looking for loot, but that's not true.

"When I ran out of the Chop House a big Caddy drew up alongside and hopped up on the curb. I jumped in beside the driver, who turned out to be Benny Siegel. He was smilin' but he said that there was so much noise he was about to come in himself.

"Benny and I went to Brooklyn and I slept like a baby," Charlie said. "The next day Mendy and I did have a sit down with Lepke, but it was not to iron out a beef, it was for congratulations and payoff. Mendy and me never had any beef about that hit or any other.

"And that's how the hit on the Dutchman went down," Charlie "The Bug" Workman said, sitting back in his chair and taking a drink of his beer. "Anybody tells you any different is full of shit."

CHAPTER 5

Fate brought my father and his pal, Johnny Spinoza, in front of a judge. My father told me about how the cops — "Bulls," he called them — used to harass him and Spinoza because the two of them had a reputation on the streets. The cops who worked the beat around the Paramount Theater liked to single the pair out because they wanted to embarrass them in front of the large crowds of bobbysoxers who gathered there to hear crooners like Sinatra. As the girls watched, the bulls would push my father and Spinoza up against the wall and frisk them.

On one such occasion my father had the misfortune of being caught carrying a piece and was arrested. He had been arrested before, but this bust would change his life forever.

In those days it wasn't difficult to get into the military. You could have a criminal record, and you could be a high school drop-out. If you were a warm body, they would take you.

Judges often dangled an enlistment option before delinquents as an alternative to the reformatory and a criminal record.

Recruiters knew this and loitered in the courthouses offering men a literal "Get out of jail free" card. My father and Spinoza were prime targets and with a word to a friendly judge, a Marine Corps recruiter was ready with everything but their shots. Before they knew it they were off to Quantico, Virginia, because the Corps had not yet established Parris Island for boot camps.

In a strange way it was in the Marine Corps that my father found his real niche in life. He would come to love the Corps and for the rest of his life lived "Semper Fi" — Always Faithful. — which is engraved on his tombstone today. He imitated the drill sergeants who turned him from a street hood into a fighting man and expected his family — me especially — to follow the code of the Corps. One of my earliest memories is as a five-year-old boy being drilled by my father at Fort Dix in New Jersey. When I see the photograph of myself as a little boy in loose-fitting fatigues, I can hear my father growling "Left Face! Right Shoulder...Aarrrrms!"

That was the beginning of my own military career and while those drills may seem strange to some, I firmly believe that what my father taught me then saved my life. Anyone who has ever been in close combat will tell you that the time they spent drilling with a bayonet was time well-spent. My father, no stranger to hand-to-hand combat, had me doing bayonet drills before I went to kindergarten. He bought me a uniform, gave me a bayonet and said "This is how you kill." By the time I was six I was as efficient with a bayonet as any special forces soldier.

My father served in the Corps from 1935 to 1942, but even after his active duty service he was connected to the military. Some of his activities are in the history books while others remain secret to this day. To my father "Omerta" — the Sicilian code of silence — applied to his work for his government as well as for things he did for the Mob. Even his closest family and friends don't know all of what he did as a member of our Armed Forces.

It is no secret that the Syndicate played an important role in America's war effort during World War II. My father's position in the Mob and as a well-trained and loyal Marine was used for the benefit of both the Mob and the government as part of "Operation Underworld."

Before the United States entered the war the country was helping sustain the British war effort with supplies. Most of these supplies crossed the Atlantic in ships that originated in the Port of New York, whose docks were fully under the control of the Syndicate. Not a crate of food or ammunition would be loaded into a cargo ship without the say-so of the gangsters who ran the longshoremen's union. While there was always a bit of profiteering by the mob, they were almost to a man loyal Americans who were proud to be a part of the war effort.

However, there were also Axis saboteurs on the docks whose motives were more sinister.

In the early days of the war German U-boats were having little trouble using Allied ships for torpedo target practice. Despite the convoy system shipping losses continued to rise. The military figured the man to speak to about the problem was Socks Lanza, who was the Mob's point man on the waterfront. The problem was how to approach him.

For several weeks the military tried the head-on approach by approaching men and asking point-blank to speak to Socks. They were met with stony stares, silence, or, at best, a response like "never heard of the guy." Even as a loyal American there was no way a guy like Socks Lanza was going to just let a few guys in uniform with lots of brass on their shoulders come in and have a sit down. Nothing against the government, but it just didn't work that way.

One night my father was "shaping up" at the docks when he saw the Navy brass trying to get in contact with Socks. Shaping up is the term used by wiseguys when they stop by to see a superior in the organization to get orders, drop off the boss's cut, to show respect, or simply to shoot the shit. My father approached the naval officers, showed his Marine military ID and offered to help them in their quest to meet the boss of the New York docks.

He told them to sit tight, that he would be back shortly. My father found Socks at his usual hangout at a shoeshine stand on Water Street, surrounded by bodyguards and other members of his crew. Because Socks was well-acquainted with my father, he agreed to meet with the Navy men. That Socks Lanza agreed to do this simply based on my father's word speaks volumes about how much respect my father had earned from his fellow mobsters. Not just anyone could walk up to a man like Socks and ask him to sit down with a couple of high-ranking government men, much less cooperate with them.

My father brought the Naval men, who included at least a couple admirals, to the shoeshine stand where Socks waited with his closest men. "Keep an eye on your car," my father told the sailors, "or it will be stripped clean by the time we get back."

The admirals, used to having men snap to whenever they approached were unnerved by response they received from Socks and his boys, my father told me. Expecting to be shown the kind of respect that a lowly seaman shows an admiral, they were instead met by icy glares and inscrutable faces.

"We would like to speak to Mr. Lanza," one of the brass said to the crew, expecting them to leave. They didn't move.

"Just say your piece," my father told the admiral.

The officer explained the problem of saboteurs on the docks and asked if Socks could help. Sipping a cup of coffee, Socks saw an opportunity to help a friend.

"I'm only the boss here," he said, referring to the Fish Market. "The guy youse need the government put away for 40 years. The only guy who can give an order like that is Charlie Luciano and he's rotting away in Dannemora."

Socks maneuvered them into a position where they would have to play ball by his rules. Simply by asking for help, by revealing their weakness, the admirals had given Socks the leverage he needed to make things better for Lucky. The Syndicate never did anything for free — not then, not now. If the Navy wanted help, it had to pay. In not so many words my father explained it to them.

"I'm a Marine," he told them, "and I know all of these guys will help you, but you gotta help them, too. You gotta help Luciano. He's the only one who can arrange this for you."

In short order, Lucky, who had been wasting away in Dannemora prison, a hell-hole near the Canadian border not fit for use as a zoo, was moved downstate where he could be closer to his pals like Meyer Lansky, Joey Adonis, and Albert Anastasia.

As an aside, it's interesting that two bosses of the same mob family, Lucky Luciano and Vito Genovese, were sent to prison on trumped-up charges. Sure, both men were mobsters who committed crimes, but the Mann Act charges that brought down Lucky were made up falsehoods supported by perjured testimony, and the drug charge that put Genovese behind bars for life were a set-up by guys who wanted him out of the way. I guess all's fair in love, war, and the mob.

So anyway, thanks to the accidental intervention of my father, Charlie Luciano ended up with a shorter prison term in a much nicer joint, sabotage on the docks was reduced, and, most importantly, lives were saved.

Charlie Luciano and the Syndicate did more for the war effort than the government would like to admit. U.S. aircraft making sorties over Sicily were marked with the letter "L" to let the people know that they were OK, and Lucky's influence with the Sicilian dons allowed for increased cooperation with the troops which made things at least a little easier for American GIs.

In 1939 the government once again benefited from my father's underworld connections. Tough Tony Anastasio was the brother of Albert A., although they spelled their last names differently. Who knows why. Tough Tony was one of my father's sponsors in the mob and would always remain one of his closest, dearest friends. In a world where friends regularly betrayed each other, Tough Tony and my father remained close and worthy of the others' trust. Like Socks in Manhattan, Tony was the boss of the Brooklyn waterfront. When he came to the city, Tony used to like to spend his time at the Alto-Knight Social Club on Mulberry Street, but he could usually be found at the ILWU headquarters on Court Street in Brooklyn. It was from there that Tony put my father to work at the shipyard as a union steward. My father was in charge of work assignments and shape-ups. The work was a real-life version of the film "On the Waterfront," which was based on events at the docks in New York Harbor.

As he worked on the docks my father said he had a feeling that something wasn't right, that there was something hooky going on with the work, but for a long time he couldn't put his finger on it. He just said that he had this feeling in the back of his head that something was wrong.

Reporting this back to Tough Tony, my father continued to watch and investigate and eventually, while he was working in the lower hull of a cargo ship he discovered that some of the men were misloading the ship by placing lighter cargo on the bottom and the heavier stuff on top. While the ship was moored nothing would seem amiss, but soon after the ship hit the blue water of the deep ocean, the motion of the waves would cause the load to shift. The listing ship would have to slow down and would thus be an easy target for the prowling U-boats. Even if the ship wasn't torpedoed, it would take longer than necessary to get the badly needed supplies to the other side of the Atlantic. My father told Tony about the activities and let's just say that the loyal longshoremen had a way of making the saboteurs pay. At the end of the war captured Nazi agents told their interrogators that it was almost impossible to cause any damage on the docks because of the "violent Italians."

CHAPTER 6

Without a doubt my father's most cherished service to his country was the time he spent in actual fighting during the Second World War. As a Marine my father went island-hopping in the Pacific until 1942 when he was wounded and given an honorable discharge. His DD-214 discharge papers, however, said his discharge was "at the convenience of the government."

Apparently the government found his discharge to be "inconvenient" because he eventually turned up in Burma as part of the 5307th Composite Unit (Provisional), better known as "Merrill's Marauders."

It is a mystery to all of us as to how this happened, because he used a different name when he served in the China-Burma-India theater than he used during his time with the Marines in the Pacific. His family has never been able to find out whether this was done with the knowledge of the government as part of an OSS operation or because my father just felt like doing it. I am inclined to think that it was an OSS operation, if only because of the type of missions my father would later admit taking part in and in his admonition as he got older that after he died we were not — under no circumstances — to look into his military career.

"After I'm gone don't look into what I had to do in the military," he said to my mother. "It will hurt many people even today."

My father was always a closed-mouth man, but when he didn't want to talk about something he just didn't talk about it. Only with his service in the latter part of the war in the Pacific did he forbid us from investigating. Because he felt so strongly about keeping secret his time in the China-Burma-India theater, I believe that there is something else to the story.

A friend of my father's who served with him in the 5307th did talk a little bit about what it was like there.

"I survived the war no thanks to your father," he told me. "He liked to volunteer us for every hazardous duty out there."

He said the other GIs called them "The Bobbsey Twins" and they remained lifelong friends, with the man serving as Best Man at my parents' wedding. Over the years I would try to get things out of him about my father but all he would tell me was something like "If you went out on R&R with your dad you could count on getting in a fight and winding up in some bathhouse in India with beautiful women washing you down.

"Whenever we went on leave your father liked to joke. 'Hold on to your wallet!'"

He and my father died within months of each other and I know that they are somewhere raising hell.

My father's work on the New York docks came in handy nearly 12,000 miles away when the British forces under the command of Lord Mountbatten were experiencing problems on the docks in India. General Stradlemeyer, my father's superior officer, assigned him to Admiral Mountbatten to assist in clearing out some kind of "bottleneck," as my father described it. Once again, my father's commitment to Omerta has come back to tease his family, because while we don't know just what he did to solve Lord Mountbatten's problem, we do have a beautiful silk cloth with the symbols of the Scottish Rite of the Freemasons embossed on it along with some mysterious writing and a message signed by Lord Mountbatten expressing his best wishes for my father. Toward the end of his life my father told me that thanks to Mountbatten, he was a 33rd Degree Mason. As far as I can tell, there is no higher honor in the Scottish Rite.

After my father's death I was contacted by an old war buddy of his who later went on to have a career with the U.S. government and with the Los Angeles Police Department. He shared a story of my father's military days right before they shipped out to India. It is proof that while my father was a loyal American soldier, he was also a wiseguy at heart.

"We had two weeks of R&R before we shipped out," the man told me (I promised to keep his name confidential for obvious reasons). "One night as we were getting close to shipping out your father asked me to go out with him and a couple of friends his from New York City.

"I was up for a major night on the town, so we headed out and ended up at this big hotel in LA. We stood around for a while and then this big Caddy pulled up and your dad's friends were inside.

"As we got into the Cadillac I thought I was gonna die because here was your dad hugging and kissing Bugsy Siegel! Here I am a cop on the LA police force working as an MP, the son of an LA cop and I'm in a car with Bugsy Siegel."

As he told me the story I thought to myself, "I hope you didn't call him Bugsy" because Ben Siegel hated that nickname and would punch anyone who uttered it to his face.

"I had another fit when from the front seat a beautiful woman, I realized later it was Virginia Hill, turned around and said, 'Hi, good looking,' to your dad.

"But wait there's more," the ex-cop told me, sounding like a TV pitchman. "The driver of the Caddy was George Raft."

He said that they all went clubbing to the best spots in Los Angeles, all the while he was having a ball but hoping he didn't run into anyone who knew him in civilian life.

"For all intents and purposes Siegel was nice, that Hill dame had a mouth like a sewer, and George Raft was all quiet-like. Bugsy was telling your dad about this place outside an Army air corps training base in the desert that had legal gambling and how they were gonna make a mint. I didn't realize it at the time, but he was talking about Las Vegas."

It was only toward the end of his life that my father would talk about his time with Merrill's Marauders. They lived through hell, fighting through deadly bouts of dysentery, dengue fever, and leeches, not to mention Burmese natives and the 18th Japanese Army.

In slightly more than five months of combat, working in six combat teams, each named after a particular color, the Marauders had advanced 750 miles through some of the harshest jungle terrain in the world, fought in five major engagements and engaged in combat with the Japanese Army on 32 separate occasions. They traversed more jungle terrain on their long-range missions than any other U.S. Army formation during World War II.

"We were crazy bastards," my father said. "We were treated unfairly and we never got the credit we deserved."

I agree that the Marauders were crazy bastards — brave, but crazy. I do think that they got recognized. The U.S. Army Ranger beret flash contains the six colors of the Marauders combat teams, and the 75th Ranger Regiment, active in 2009, can trace its history back to the 5307th Composite Unit.

After the war my father returned to New York City and to the life he knew before the military. My father only talked about combat once, and that was toward the end of his life. He was sitting in a chair and suddenly said to my mother, "In Burma, the first Jap I killed during an ambush. I went over to check him out for papers and he was still alive.

"He pointed to his pocket and I took out a picture of a woman. I placed it to his lips and he kissed it and then died," my father continued. "I'm a killer."

He had never talked as openly before.

CHAPTER 7

My father remained a part of the reserves and loved the Corps until the day he died, but at heart he was a man of the streets. Organized crime had matured in the years after Prohibition ended and was becoming the operation we are all familiar with. There were the five families that would evolve into the Bonanno, Lucchese, Genovese, Gambino, and Columbo borgatas although most of them were known by different names at the time. For example, the group known today as the Columbo family was headed then by Joe Profaci; this borgata would have a profound influence in my own life years later, but that is a story for another day.

The borgata known today as the Gambino family was under the control of Phil Mangano, who would soon be displaced by my father's friend, Albert Anastasia — at the time the underboss. When he returned to the United States, my father reported to Anastasia.

What we call today the Genovese family was founded by Lucky Luciano, who relinquished much of the control of the operation to his boyhood friend Frank Costello after Charlie was convicted of pandering charges and deported to Sicily after the war. The family's second-in-command, or underboss, was Vito Genovese, but one of Costello's closest allies was Anthony Carfano, who was known on the street as Little Augie Pisano. I knew the man as Gussie, and he was my grandfather.

With a six-inch scar on his cheek, a souvenir from a long-forgotten knife fight, Augie Pisano was a well-known racketeer who was no stranger to front page headlines because of his activities in controlling unions and his influence in the garment trade, but to me he was no different than anyone else's grandfather. It just turns out that when my grandfather died it was front-page news in every paper in New York City. I don't know of too many other children who learn that their grandfather was "rubbed out, mob-style" with one bullet in the neck, another in the forehead and more than $2,000 in cash in his pocket.

While I do have fond memories of Gussie as a doting grandfather, it was as a mobster that my strongest memory of him is etched in my mind. I was just a young boy, a smart-ass, really, when the phone rang at my grandfather's palatial home in Queens. I picked it up and although the connection was filled with static, I knew immediately who it was once the gravelly voice came through the receiver in response to my query, "Who is this?"

"Who is dis?" came the response. I told him who I was.

"Ah," said Lucky Luciano. "So, when you grow up do you want to be like your grandfather or your dad?"

"Maybe I'll be like you, Mr. Luciano," I replied.

"Are you a wiseguy?" he asked.

"Only if you say so," I said.

"Get your fuckin' grandfather on the phone," he said, apparently tiring of speaking to a wiseass little punk like me. "I'm calling from Italy."

I decided to have a little fun. "I thought you were in Cuba," I said. In response I got a stream of Italian cursing. I quickly gave the phone to my grandfather.

After they talked privately Gussie came to me and gave me a playful slap to the cheek (that only smarted a little) and said "you never talk to a boss like that." Then he laughed.

It wasn't until I was much older and more experienced with mob matters that I learned there was a good chance that phone was bugged by the feds and that joking about something like where Lucky was located was really not a smart thing to do.

From before the time that my father was born on the kitchen floor of his tenement near the bridge, my grandfather was involved in the rackets. He had worked his way up through the ranks and was particularly close to Frank Costello and Joey Adonis. They, in turn, entrusted some of their most important business to him.

One of the traits he had, that he passed on to his sons, and that my father passed on to me was loyalty. He was fiercely faithful to his friends and in the end this probably cost him his life. His loyalty to Frank Costello made him a threat to fellow mobster Vito Genovese, and the fact that he himself was incapable of betrayal made him blind to the first, most important lesson a mobster can never forget: beware of your friends — if you are going to be hit, they will very likely have something to do with it.

The story of how Vito Genovese hired Chin Gigante to shoot Frank Costello so that Vito could take over the borgata is one of the most famous in the history of American crime, so I won't bother to recite it here. Suffice to say that in 1957 Genovese wanted control of Costello's operations and attempted to have him killed. When the attempt failed Genovese summoned all of the important lieutenants in the family to report to him because he feared reprisal. Only one man remained loyal to Costello — my grandfather. His refusal to report to Genovese's New Jersey mansion infuriated Vito and he never forgot the snub.

When Costello stepped aside for Genovese, one of the conditions was "amnesty" for Little Augie. The peaceful transition from Costello to Genovese was unusual enough that perhaps everyone that the equally strange idea of forgiveness of Augie's disrespect would work out as well. That, of course, was a silly idea, and Genovese simply bided his time until Augie could be hit.

How and why my grandfather was murdered is another one of those famously inaccurate mob stories. Everyone thinks it was a revenge killing ordered by Genovese because of the Costello deal. It wasn't. Not only that, but it has always been believed that Tony Bender, a Genovese capo whose real name was Anthony Strollo, helped put the finger on his good friend. Not so.

It is important that history be written accurately, even if it is the history of a mob hit. So here is the true reason of why and how my grandfather was murdered. As far as I know this, like the Dutch Schultz killing Charlie the Bug told me about, has never been accurately reported anywhere.

For my grandfather, times had changed in the Syndicate. He could only speak to his old friend Lucky periodically through the static of a transatlantic telephone call, his friend Albert Anastasia was dead, Frank Costello was in semi-retirement, and his hated rival, Vito Genovese was in control of the Luciano borgata. In addition, my grandfather was no spring chicken and was looking for a change.

He saw a golden opportunity in Florida, which at the time was nearly uncharted territory. Little Augie especially liked Miami and Miami Beach, so he began to move in on the rackets there. In doing so he ran afoul of a pair of very influential men: Meyer Lansky and Santo Trafficante. Meyer also coveted Miami, with its closeness to Cuba, where he was running casinos for the Cuban dictator Batista. Trafficante was operating out of Tampa, which was a big narcotics hub. Trafficante, Lansky, and Genovese were not particularly close — in fact Trafficante and Lansky were almost at war over the east coast of Florida — but they put aside their differences to put a stop to my grandfather's actions in Florida.

Genovese, who was my grandfather's boss, had to approve the hit, which he did without a second thought. The only question remaining was how.

My grandfather did not survive a half-century in organized crime by being careless, so the commonly held belief that he was whacked by gunmen whom he did not see sitting in the back of his Cadillac is crazy. He taught me that no matter how rushed a guy was ALWAYS check the backseat AND the trunk of the car. I remember this lesson vividly. My grandfather was a gunman, he knew how to carry out a hit and he knew how to protect himself. There is no way that a hitman could hide in the backseat of a car and take out my grandfather.

The "fact" that Tony Bender was the hitman is also a load of crap. We know that the guys who killed Little Augie were from Joey Adonis's crew. Tony was a friend of my grandfather, that's true, but in this case the hit didn't come from him — it came from another friend.

On September 29, 1959, my grandfather was out with a friend, Janice Drake, who, interestingly had been with Albert A. the night before he was whacked. She might have been bad luck, but Janice had nothing to do with my grandfather's death. They were also with Tony Bender. Earlier, my father had warned his dad that he was the target of a hit, but Augie thought he was untouchable and said so.

While the group was eating, my grandfather received a phone call from Meyer Lansky. We are pretty sure that Lansky told him he wanted to discuss the Florida situation in person. Whether my grandfather expected to meet directly with Meyer or with one of his representatives is unknown. Regardless, Augie and Janice left the restaurant and were not heard from again until they were discovered dead in Augie's Cadillac not far from La Guardia Airport. The story goes that they were surprised by gunmen hiding in the backseat and forced to drive to the place where they were shot. That's not true.

My family learned later that Augie was lured to the spot and was gunned down by shooters from Joey Adonis's crew. Janice Drake had to die because she saw the gunmen. She was just in the wrong place at the wrong time and now she's forever linked to one of the most famous hits in mob history.

I am sure that when my grandfather saw the guys approaching he knew them and was temporarily off-guard. I am also sure that it didn't take him long to realize that this was a hit and that his number was up. He probably was not surprised that he knew the men who were going to kill him. After all, that's always the way it happens.

My grandfather's death made headlines in New York City and there was lots of speculation about why it happened. Because of his chosen lifestyle, the Archdiocese refused to let him be buried in consecrated ground. However, in 1961 his body was quietly moved to a mausoleum belonging to some relatives in a Catholic cemetery. It is likely that this was done without the knowledge of the Church because the cemetery records regarding the transfer are incomplete. Chances are the cemetery caretaker was swayed by a wad of bills to look the other way. I have visited his grave and it looks like a peaceful place. I'm glad that Gussie is resting with his family. He deserves no less.

After I was featured on a Biography Channel television show about Murder, Inc., I received a telephone call claiming to be my cousin from Little Augie's side of the family through marriage. The guy's name was DeSalvio, which is the name on the tomb where my grandfather is laid to rest. It was nice to hear from someone who wanted to get together as cousins, considering that on the Trager side, all we have are Willie's survivors and I've already said how I feel about them.

CHAPTER 8

I never started out to write a book about my father until I realized what he had given to me and to my soul. In many ways he made me grow up before my time, and made me different than other kids growing up. I don't know many other preschoolers who know close order drills or how to handle a bayonet. From my father I learned how to shake down a person with a few choice words.

He had me baptized by a man whose name I will only mention in the acknowledgments in this book as I loved him. This man schooled me in the street and in the true ways of the world. When I was coming home from Vietnam he was coming home from prison. I had just a short but valuable time with him before he was gunned down in the early morning hours outside a clam bar on Mulberry Street in Little Italy. This man taught me to fight with words, then he helped a high-school dropout, part-time truck driver and singer in local nightclubs go through college and law school.

But I'm getting ahead of myself.

At 16, I quit school and got a job as a Teamster with an airport-based trucking company. Family friends Johnny Dio and Harry

Davidoff, two of the bigger names in the New York underworld, got me the job. Dio was best known for his appearance before the McClellan Commission when, under questioning by committee counsel Robert F. Kennedy, he took the Fifth 146 times. The McClellan Commission referred to Davidoff, who spent time behind bars for extortion and tax evasion, as "a ruthless thug."

By this time, I had earned the moniker "Frankie 13," given to me by numbers customers who considered me to be good luck.

"You're my good luck charm," one winner told me as I delivered his winnings.

"Yeah, lucky 13," muttered a friend, who was less fortunate. The name stuck.

"Here comes Frankie 13," they'd laugh as I came to pick up cash or, less frequently, to pay off winners.

In the trucking company, my mentor was a man named Tony Bernardo. His friends liked to call him "Cockhound." The name fit. On one of my first jobs Tony and I picked up a shipment of jackets at the docks and prepared to load them for delivery.

"We gotta count 'em," Tony said, after slipping a bribe to the shipping clerk between the bills of lading.

Tony proceeded to open the boxes of jackets and began sifting through the soon-to-be swag.

"Here's one box," he said, taking five jackets out.

"Here's another," I replied, lifting a pair.

By the time we delivered the shipment to a local department store, we had liberated about a grand worth of jackets.

On the side, I had a singing career that was progressing nicely. I not only could sing the traditional Italian songs the old guys liked to hear, but I was up on the current hits of guys like Dion, Frankie Avalon and, of course, Sinatra. In addition, Frankie 13, as I was known on the stage, was a competent trumpet player, too. I studied classic voice with Carlo Menotti, who taught me the technique of singing the Neapolitan songs favored by wiseguys.

My big break came one night in the San Susan, a wiseguy-frequented nightclub on Long Island, where performers like Bobby Darin, Jerry Vale and Steve Lawrence would play. The San Susan held a "Roman

Feast" which featured all-you-can-eat pasta and soup dishes which was popular not only with racketeers, but with the general public as well. The house band at the time was Joe Martin and his orchestra whose performance, I recall, left a lot to be desired.

One evening, with the very important Joe Colombo in attendance, Martin's singer quit the orchestra shortly before show time.

"Joe, we got a problem," said Vic (One-Arm) Amuso, who was running the joint. "We got no act."

Joe looked around and saw me, whom he had heard sing before.

"We gotta have a singer," Joe said to Vic.

"Frankie!" he called to me. "Go across the street and buy yourself a tux and whatever else you need."

The celebrity mob boss and Italian civil rights leader handed me a wad of bills. He then turned very serious and his eyes grew narrow as he swept a strand of his thinning hair from in front of his face.

"I'm gonna tell you something," Colombo said. "One of two things is gonna happen tonight. If you sing good, you can keep the tux. If you don't do good, we'll bury you in it."

That was Joe's way. He liked me; he did not intend to kill me, he just wanted me to understand the seriousness of the situation. Reputation was important to these men and Joe Colombo wanted me to recognize that he had enough confidence to put his own reputation on the line.

For the next hour-and-a-half, dressed in a tux complete with mauve shirt with ruffled cuffs and collar, I belted my heart out with songs like "Mala Femmena" and other Neapolitan classics.

Joe Colombo loved my performance, but for me, the best moment of the night came when Jimmy Roselli, the second-most famous singer from Hoboken, sent me a Courvoisier as a salute. The night at the San Susan led to a signing with an agent and performances in the Catskills. I played the Copa, appearing on the marquee with such names as Rosemary Clooney and Frankie Avalon, and at Grossingers.

Me beneath the Williamsburg Bridge.

The DeSalvi Mausoleum where Anthony Carfano
was re-interred two years after the Catholic Church
denied him burial in a Catholic cemetery.

Me and Raymond, one of my friends and contacts in Chinatown.

My father during his service with the U.S. Marine Corps.

Me during my heyday as a public defender.

This is a photo of me taken at Fort Dix
during my "training" by my father.

I was called up to active duty in New York Harbor within hours of the terrorist attacks on September 11, 2001.

My father and a friend pose for the camera somewhere in the China/Burma/India theater during their service with Merrill's Marauders.

A wall of memories in a friend's restaurant. Most of these
pictures show President Street in Brooklyn, where a war
between two factions of a mob family took place.

Even in the days after 9/11 I remember the men
who did not come home from Vietnam.

My father and a friend in the Marine Corps.

My father and me at the grave of his uncle Jake Trager.

My Chinese brother Leon, who taught me how
to survive in the streets of Chinatown.

"Baby John the Cannoli King"
with
Ryan Seacrest from American Idol

Italian Pastries • Pizza • Imported Desserts
Panini Sandwiches • Espresso Bar
Beer • Wine • Cocktails

Caffe' Palermo
148 Mulberry St. N.Y., N.Y. 10013
(212)431-4205
www.CaffePalermo.com

Baby John DeLutro's Caffe' Palermo is a must-see stop in Little Italy. Here he poses with Ryan Seacrest of "American Idol."

CHAPTER 9

My write up and picture — a mustachioed Italian recording artist whose looks belied his young age — appeared in the New York papers, including a mention in the all-important Ed Sullivan Talk of the Town column. I cut a record, "My Boy" — later covered by Elvis — and was on his way as the record moved up to number 100 nationally.

However, when I turned 18, my 1-A draft status put an end to my show business career.

The draft notice could not have come at a worse time. I had just recorded a demo of "Hey There, Lonely Girl" which had won approval from the powers-that-be at Roulette Records. It could have been the break-through song I needed to make the big time. Unfortunately, at that time, artists needed to be able to tour to promote their singles and being a recording artist was not sufficient to earn a draft deferment. Instead, "Lonely Girl" was given to another up-and-coming singer, Eddie Holman, whose version hit the charts and made him a star.

Sitting in the mess hall of the Brooklyn military induction center having just completed and passed my draft physical, I was still pretty lit from the remnants of a previous 24-hour bender. The MPs stationed in the center had done a good job of finding most of the booze I had stashed on me to continue the party, but they hadn't found all of it. It was 1970 and the army was happy to take just about any potential draftee who had enough brains to walk through the door. Drunk or sober, it was clear that I was going into the service that day. Then some hard-ass army top-kick said I was too loaded to get sworn-in and he ordered me to go to the center's canteen to sober up.

The sergeant sent me upstairs, after doing his best to confiscate the booze and told me to come back in four hours, when the next group would be ready for induction.

"And you better be sober," he warned.

The mess was filled with more uniforms than I had ever seen outside the Veterans Day parades and with most of them belonging to recruiters, they were sharp and covered with a lot of brass. One of the uniformed men stood out. In his dress whites, the Coast Guard Chief Petty Officer looked like Merv Griffin.

"Hey! Merv," I called drunkenly. "Will you put me in the show?"

The chief came over looked at me with a mixture of bemusement and scorn.

"What're you doing up here?" he asked with the authority of a CPO.

"I wanna serve our country," I said. "I'm just waiting to get called up by the army."

The chief laughed.

"Army! What the hell do you want to join the army for? You should be in the Coast Guard."

"The Coast Guard? You mean like lifeguards and that?" I asked.

"Not exactly," the chief said. "But it beats the hell out of the army and all that marching."

"I could do four years patrolling Jones Beach easy," Frank said.

"At worst they'll send you to Sandy Hook," the chief winked, knowing he had hooked a fish.

The chief didn't care whether I was sober or not.

"I can swear you in right now," he said.

And he did.

After the Marines, the toughest, most grueling boot camp belongs to the U.S. Coast Guard. Not technically a branch of the Defense Department, the Coast Guard is, in peacetime, responsible for police-type actions: hunting down and stopping smugglers and protecting the inland waterways and lakes from dangerous and clueless boaters. In wartime, the U.S. Coast Guard likes to call itself the rock-hard core around which the Navy forms. For most of the enlistees like me, there would be no patrols in a cutter outside Jones Beach. Rather, without realizing it, I had volunteered for some of the most hazardous duty in Southeast Asia.

This possibility hadn't dawned on me until I completed boot camp and received my orders to report aboard the Dallas, a Coast Guard High-Endurance Cutter stationed in Subic Bay, Philippines.

Within a couple of days, as a "D.I.E." or draft-induced enlistment, I made my way 12,000 miles around the world and was aboard the Dallas when she received orders to take part in Operation Market Time.

Most Americans are familiar with the Ho Chi Minh Trail, the supply lines that kept the North Vietnamese army and Viet Cong armed and fed. The trail ran down from North Vietnam and the Central Highlands to the Mekong River Delta in southern Vietnam. However, Vietnam is a country filled with rivers, canals and small waterways that make it look like the Venice of the Far East. Charlie was just as able to supply his troops in the south via the water as he was through the Ho Chi Minh Trail. Until Market Time, the U.S. had no smaller ships capable of shutting down these inland supply routes. Marines on land could merely stand and fire in frustration as the motorized junks moved Chinese-made weapons down the Ong Doc and Mekong rivers. The Americans turned to the Navy, which in turn ordered the Coast Guard, with its PBRs, swiftboats and cutters, into the South Thailand Sea to shut down the water-based supply routes.

Casualties in Market Time were high. The Viet Cong and NVA didn't just turn over the waterways when the Americans showed up and Frank was soon ordered ashore at the base at Song Ong Doc, a military staging area for Riverines, Special Forces, Seals and the Coast

Guard at the mouth of the Ong Doc River. Song Ong Doc, which rolls off the tongue sounding more like "sunna duck", was a floating tactical support base made up of six large barges moored on the Ong Doc River in Ca Mau Province, a VC stronghold.

As a gunner on a WPG, I saw a lot of action. My WPG was involved in several search and rescue operations near An Thoi and Song Ong Doc and fighting in the area was heavy. A WPG was a high-speed craft, about 80 feet long. WPGs were heavily armed; they carried two-.50-caliber guns forward, an M-60 machine gun and an M-18 grenade launcher, and an additional .50-caliber machine gun aft.

One mission I'll remember to the day I die occurred shortly after I arrived in-country. I was manning a .50 on a WPG when we started taking fire from a village near the river.

"Bari!" my skipper shouted. "Fire for effect!"

That meant open fire with everything you have and I did so in what we called a "mad minute." Eventually the gun started to cook off, which means that it got so hot that the shells were firing on their own accord. The only way to stop a machine gun that is cooking is to cut the ammo belt.

Once the machine gun stopped firing, I looked at what was left of the village. There was nothing there. Then something caught my eye; rolling down toward the river was a child's red ball. It was the same kind of ball I had played with back in the City when I was a kid. That meant that there had been children in that village. The best-case scenario for me was that I destroyed that kid's home. I didn't want to think about the worst-case scenario.

There were down times in Song Ong Doc, and I took advantage of the quiet days to get to know the area around the base, which included a nearby orphanage run by Buddhist monks. Much of my off-duty time was taken up in what the grunts called I&I - intoxication and intercourse.

I later spent time with a helicopter search and rescue squad, doing long-range patrols and special forces insertions. I returned to the United States and finished my active duty tour with the Coast Guard.

When I returned to Brooklyn, I was an older, more thoughtful person, but I was plagued with flashbacks and Vietnam nightmares - something that continues to this day. It isn't unusual for me to wake up in a cold sweat from dreams of Task Force 115, Coast Guard Squadron 3, the guys from the 9th Infantry Division that we supported. I see the faces of guys I served with, some of whom never came home, and others who came home, but who really never left Vietnam. To this day I wear an MIA/POW pin in honor of my brothers who have not yet come home.

CHAPTER 10

My godfather's death had a profound impact on me. It made me take a long, hard look at my life and where it was going. Organized crime was a one-way ticket to oblivion, I decided, and I began to distance myself from that life. I went back to school, got my GED, and thanks to the GI Bill, enrolled in St. Johns University, planning on a law career.

For the first time in my life, I was interested in the future, looking for security and peace. I wanted to contribute something good to society.

I was admitted to the bar in New York and New Jersey and took a job with the public defender's office in Essex County, New Jersey before coming back over the George Washington Bridge to work as an 18-b lawyer in New York City.

As a public defender in Newark I was assigned parole hearings in Rahway Prison. My office was a cell. I liked it; it was cozy, especially during riots when I would get locked in. I started to enjoy the jail food of bologna sandwiches on white bread, but the Kool-aid they served gave me 'Nam flashbacks. I went to a shrink who gave me tranquilizers to get through it.

As a public defender I also represented people in arraignment courts. I remember one client who had raped a girl and as the prosecutor was reading the indictment I was concentrating on what I had to do. I snapped out of it as the judge gave a shout of surprise — my client was masturbating in open court. He blew his load before I realized what was going on. When I asked him why he did that he told me he had gotten excited when the female prosecutor was reading the details of his crime. Needless to say we accepted a plea deal.

Defending rapists was, unfortunately, a regular duty. The public defender's office had a psychiatrist on staff who had to evaluate our clients and this clearly upset him. He took more tranquilizers than I did. He was a nice, gentle guy, with a small son. Every time he evaluated a sex offender it was clear that he was repulsed. He would wash his hands over and over after an evaluation. Eventually he committed suicide. That shows you how messed up public defense law is: the staff psychiatrist was suicidal.

Attorneys are supposed to zealously defend their clients' rights, regardless of the guilt or innocence of the client. Often defense attorneys are forced to take on clients that they find personally repugnant. I had to justify to myself how I could defend such people; I did so by realizing that the Constitution must apply to all people or it will apply to no one. My father fought to defend this and so did I. I owed it to him to do the best I could.

I had one client assigned at arraignment. When I first met him in the holding cell, his head was bandaged and he was badly bruised. His story was that he was waiting for a bus when he was approached by a woman whom he said was a prostitute. She offered her services and he declined. She got angry and yelled "Rape!" Her pimp came by and beat him up. He was released when the state's case fell apart.

As I investigated his background I discovered that he was involved with the Scared Straight program that had been developed at Rahway. He had been sentenced to 15 years for a rape that occurred at the same spot where he was arrested this time but was eventually paroled by mistake by the New Jersey Parole Board. Having realized its mistake the Parole Board wanted him back inside and used his latest arrest to rescind his parole and send him back to Rahway. In doing so they violated his right to due process of law, which says that everyone has the right to the full legal process before their freedom is taken away. Again, if the government does that to the worst kind of criminal, it won't be long before they do it to others.

I fought the Parole Board all the way up to the New Jersey Supreme Court and eventually won a decision that requires the state to follow due process before revoking parole. This meant that this guy had to be released from Rahway.

Unfortunately, sex offenders rarely are rehabilitated and this guy was no exception. Shortly after his release there occurred a series of rapes in 13th Avenue Park, which is where my client had had all of his trouble. I confronted him about this and he just started shaking. He denied it, but I knew it was him.

One day while I was sitting outside arraignment court, some Essex County detectives came by with a warrant for this guy's arrest. He had been identified by seven victims. I told them that I would bring him in. I found him, but he refused to accompany me and left. Several days later I was watching television as a SWAT team converged on my client's home. As I watched I received a telephone call. It was my client. He was standing outside his house at a nearby telephone booth and he was wondering what he should do. The SWAT team had surrounded his home but was ignorant of the fact that the guy they wanted was right under their noses. I told him to surrender peacefully, but once again he refused. I saw him walk away from the scene right on TV.

He was captured a few days later in the act of assaulting a woman at the park. When I finally got to speak to him I asked him why he was drawn to that spot. He told me he was impotent except at that park. My investigator, another attorney and I walked around the area, but none of us got aroused. To this day I don't understand what that spot in the park did for him.

Eventually I left the public defender's office to go out on my own. I joined what New York State calls the "18-b panel," named for the section of the court rules that allows for private attorneys to receive assignments as state-paid public defenders.

Eighteen-b lawyers are the grunts of the New York legal profession. Similar to public defenders, 18-b lawyers take clients who cannot be represented by the PD's office because of conflicts of interest that arise out of having multiple defendants brought up for the same offense. The career expectancy of an 18-b attorney is short, much like that of a galley slave back in the days of the Roman Empire. There are always new lawyers coming up to take the place of the ones who burn up, die or just plain quit. They waste away or flame out because most of the time, they are forced to hang around the basement holding cells of the courthouse, a place that looks like it was conceived by Hieronymus Bosch and produced by Salvatore Dali.

The holding cells of 100 Centre Street, where the accused criminals not out on bail await court appearances, have, at first glance the appearance of chaos. This what Dante must have envisioned when he conceived his Inferno: the stench of fear, madness, sorrow, guilt, anger and just about every other negative emotion that humans have created lingers here, mixing with the physical odor of sweat, smoke, puke, urine and filth. There is no hope here. If there is joy, it is the false joy a lunatic experiences when he sees the full moon. It is the midpoint in a criminal's descent from reality to oblivion.

The holding cells are the epitome of the eponymous. They hold people. When you are put in a holding cell, you wait. And wait. When you are done waiting, they make you wait some more. When you think that you can't bear another minute of waiting, then you are almost done with the beginning of your wait. There is no hurry here. No one who is locked in here has anyplace better to be. They may think they do and everyone wishes they do, but they don't.

There is no serenity in these holding cells. The scary part about being in a Centre Street holding cell is when you think you have achieved some sort of peace and serenity, you begin to doubt your sanity. If you think you can take it, then there's a good chance you've lost it.

Danger is ubiquitous in a Centre Street cell. Trust no one. The guy who wants to be your friend wants information to save his own ass. The guy who will protect you, well, there ain't no such thing as a free lunch in here, baby. The guy who needs protection, he's got some serious enemies and you better stay the hell away from him, too. People who need anything in a holding cell are dangerous. They exude their need like a sick fish sends out signals to sharks and sometimes in the feeding frenzy, even healthy fish get eaten. Existing in a holding cell is like trying escape from a paradox. Don't look at anybody, you just might attract attention. But keep your eyes open, be alert at all times. In the end it's best to just stake out a section of concrete and sit your ass down, you're going to be here awhile.

Defendants who use 18-b attorneys are a sorry lot. By definition they are destitute — you don't get a court-appointed lawyer unless you can't afford to hire your own counsel — and by circumstance they are desperate. Chances are they can't post bail and are so low ranking in their alleged criminal enterprise that they have no information with which they can bargain their way out of jail time. They are the justice system's equivalent of cannon fodder.

By contrast, 18-b attorneys can be some of the most shrewd, creative and hard-working lawyers in the courthouse. They have to be. In the worst-case scenario their clients are guilty as charged, in a best case, they're probably guilty of something else. More often than not, an 18-b attorney can't trust that his client is telling them the whole truth. The 18-b clients, following the adage that you get what you pay for, don't like to listen to what their attorney tell them. It takes a very strong lawyer to get the client to shut up, answer questions and follow directions.

My clients, all near and dear to me, included the criminally insane, the indigents, the street people whose lives are bizarre, to put it bluntly. I also worked with Asian street gangs. I related to all of them. I found a comfort zone in the insanity of criminal law. I finally felt at home. I wasn't the rich kid, do-gooder that you often find in criminal law. With me it was "There but for the grace of God, go I."

My office was a cell phone, beeper, and a car. I had a regular exterminator for my car because I tended to spend much of my time in it. I ate there, met clients there; I would meet them on street corners and alleyways. Case files and paper accumulated in my car.

It sounds crazy, but it worked for me. My upbringing and my service in Vietnam affected the way I practiced law. I started fighting my cases as though I was fighting the war and for those who did not come back. I was fighting for my friends who were dying from the Agent Orange poisons in their bodies, and for those who were dying because of the demons in their heads. Everything I had been through was beginning to haunt me. I suffered from crying jags and temper tantrums and I was drinking way too much. I realized that I needed help and thankfully I got it and the medication that has helped me carry on. Unfortunately it never really goes away.

CHAPTER 11

Sometimes, no matter how hard I tried, I couldn't convince my client to follow my instructions. When a case was unwinnable, I advised my clients to cut a deal and run. Sometimes they took my advice, sometimes not. Despite having no case, some of them insisted that they wanted "a fucking trial." I didn't have a choice, so we would go to trial.

In one such case the prosecution had overwhelming evidence against my client. He had confessed, the state had eight witnesses who would put him at the scene, there were even fingerprints. But he wanted his trial.

So here was the state of New York, spending upwards of $80 an hour on jurors, $40 an hour for me to defend him, another forty bucks for the assistant DA and God only knows how much for the judge, bailiff and courtroom staff to give this guy his constitutional right to be convicted by a jury of his peers who had the misfortune to register to vote in the County of New York.

When it came time for summation, I couldn't think of one thing to say. I couldn't think of a single thing that would create even a possibility of reasonable doubt.

"I think I'm fucked," said my client.

"You think?" I replied.

The judge yelled at me. "Mr. Bari, your summation, please!"

I stood up and said the only thing that came to mind: "Mary had a little lamb, its fleece was white as snow, and everywhere that Mary went, the lamb was sure to go." I became dramatic in reciting this child's poem. When I was finished, I sat down in the silent courtroom.

"Mr. Bari, are you finished?" The judge asked.

I jumped up and yelled, "If you think that was a fairy tale, wait until you hear what the prosecutor has to tell you!"

My client applauded and the jury laughed. They convicted him and now he's doing a 40-year stretch.

I had one client with a long history of drug abuse who was in the late stages of AIDS. He was another one of those who wanted his day in court. I was questioning him gently as he was rather fragile.

It had been a straightforward bust. He had hired a hooker to give him a blow job and while they were in an abandoned car they were stopped by the cops. A search of the car turned up some drugs. My client claimed that they belonged to the hooker.

Guilt didn't matter to me. My client was a human and an American and he had civil rights just like everybody else. It boiled down to my duty as an attorney to my client. I was being paid to do the best job I could and that was that.

The problem was he hadn't given me anything to work with. When you get caught getting head from a hooker and the cops find crack, you're going to get convicted.

Putting a guilty defendant on the stand presents an ethical problem for a defense attorney. First, you can't ask the guy to incriminate himself. Second, you can't ask him to lie. Of course, the defense doesn't have to present any kind of case, they just need to show the reasonable doubt apparent in the prosecution's case. But this guy wanted to testify.

I had cross-examined the cop, she testified fairly and honestly, and there had been no holes in her story. The witnesses - all cops - had corroborated her tale of the bust. The only question the jury had to decide was whether the stash was my client's.

I finished with direct and went back to the defense table. There wasn't anything else I could do with the witness.

This Assistant DA with no trial experience stood up and shuffled his papers. He was all gung-ho. The young man cleared his throat, jerked his head with some sort of a tic and looked at my client.

"Sir, you claim you were inside this automobile to have sex with a woman, is that true?"

My client looked right at the young DA and their eyes locked. He did not reply to the question.

"Your honor, would you please direct the defendant to answer the question?" he asked. The judge did so.

The prosecutor pursed his lips, looked at my client, then to the jury and finally back to the defendant. It was almost like everyone was moving in slow motion.

My client appeared to be deep in thought, his eyes locked on the prosecutor. Then his eyes rolled back into his head so only the whites were showing. To courtroom observers, it appeared as if he was looking at the ceiling for the answer, but then he just kept leaning back further and further until his chin was perpendicular to the floor. At that moment, the chair flipped backward and he disappeared from view.

He fell to the floor with a loud crash.

Then there was silence. No one in the courtroom moved, waiting for my client to stand up and explain what the hell was going on. But he didn't. Ten seconds went by and he didn't get up. Twenty seconds and then the bailiff slowly, carefully moved in front of the bench to the witness box. The bailiff peered over and looked down. No one else in the courtroom moved, uttered a sound or breathed. Waiting.

"Uh...Judge..."

The bailiff went around to the entrance of the witness box and knelt down. Then he stood up. He knelt back down and then stood up again. In disbelief, he came to the front of the court room to stand before the judge.

"Judge, this guy's dead."

I jumped up from the defense table.

"Mistrial!" I yelled. Then I turned to that gung-ho DA, who was white as a ghost. "Great job, what a killer cross."

I counted it as a victory; after all, the guy wasn't convicted. I heard that the prosecutor quit the DA's office soon after.

I was less successful with a client I like to call "Diapers."

Everyone knows about how prison inmates file all sorts of frivolous lawsuits because they don't have anything better to do, but not many people realize that some criminals like to use the criminal justice system for fun and entertainment. Diapers was one of those guys.

I was the third lawyer this guy had. The other two asked for reassignments because they were afraid of him. He had a record as long as a day in Lent and was charged with robbery. Again it was a solid case against my client. He knew he was going back to jail, but he decided that he wanted to have some fun first. He wanted a trial to play games with the society that he blamed for ruining his life.

I called him Diapers because he liked to wear them. He said they were the only things that didn't make his hemorrhoids worse. He came into court each day complaining about his piles and once asked for an adjournment because his hemorrhoids were bleeding. To prove the truthfulness of his statement, he pulled out a piece of bloody toilet paper. I probably could have asked for a mistrial, but it's hard to get one when the defendant causes the problem. He was convicted and sentenced to 12-to-25 years.

I represented a woman who was a mule for a Colombian drug cartel. I ended up getting her a five-year term and deportation to Colombia. Once before a procedural hearing I visited her in the holding cell at Centre Street. She was the only woman in her cell. As we talked, she grabbed my hand and put it down her pants. Then she grabbed my penis and started massaging it. She was telling me she loved me, that she was very rich in Colombia and that she wanted me to come live with her there. All I could see at the time was me with a Colombian necktie, but now as I fight my clients for my meager legal fees, I wonder if I made a mistake.

CHAPTER 12

Not all of my cases were humorous, of course. One kid I'll never forget was Derrick Smith.

It was supposed to be just another plea deal. The goddamned Rockefeller drug laws killed Derrick Smith just as surely as if Nelson himself had pushed the teen out the window. Ten years earlier, Derrick would have been a candidate for alternative sentencing, but the war on drugs had claimed another casualty.

Derrick wasn't a saint, but he didn't have to die. He was just another 19-year-old, the same age I was when I shipped out, but Derrick wouldn't have a chance to redeem himself. He never really had a chance; not before he was arrested and certainly not after. He was just a poor kid from uptown trying to stay alive in the jungle of Harlem.

He had been busted before on a small drug sales charge and served part of a six-month jail term on Rikers followed by a probation term, but he was never violent. Derrick spent most of his time on the streets selling pot, which wasn't covered under the harsh mandatory minimums. He had been convicted a couple of times for selling marijuana and had his probation extended and fines assessed.

When he was arrested this time, he had been taken to Rikers Island to be held until he posted bail, but no one had been able to raise the $2,500 cash to get him out. That had been six months ago, and chances are Derrick had had a little too much taste of what was awaiting him upstate.

I had been honest with him from the outset. He had been arrested for selling crack, and the amount he sold was enough to trigger the tough sentences that the Rockefeller anti-drug laws demanded. There were very few options. The judge's hands were tied; I could go to the proffer sessions with the DA, but Derrick had nothing to offer in return. He was so low down the food chain in his drug gang that he couldn't turn and give them anybody with any authority. It was a case, frankly, that wasn't worth anyone's time. Derrick would have to plead - they had him dead-to-rights selling crack to a cop - and then he would go away. Six months or so in Rikers before he went to Butler on Staten Island, or maybe even a minimum security prison like Bayview to serve the rest of a four to six year term.

Four to six years: 1,460 to 2,190 days. To a college student, perhaps, that doesn't sound like a lot of time, but Derrick Smith was no frat boy. He was a high school dropout who had trouble reading and didn't like the school regimen. He liked hanging on the streets with his buds, playing basketball, drinking a cold 40-ouncer or gin and juice, singing rap and hiding his gang affiliation from his mother, a hardworking single mom who was doing her best not to get left behind in the economic boom of the 1990s.

Derrick looked at four years like it was a life sentence. He knew what he could expect in prison. He wasn't tough enough to stay alive even in a "safe, stable, and humane" environment like Bayview.

A few weeks prior, I met with Derrick to discuss his grand jury appearance and noticed Derrick was visibly upset. I asked the staff at Rikers to put Derrick under a suicide watch, but no one there seems to remember anybody doing anything about it.

When the day for Derrick's plea came, I managed to wrangle a shorter sentence from a sympathetic prosecutor, but all he could get was three-and-a-half to five years.

Supreme Court Judge Budd G. Goodman was a fair, but serious judge. He didn't like mandatory minimums any more than any other judge, but he was powerless to help Derrick. When he looked over Derrick's file, he didn't like what he saw. Here was a convicted criminal, albeit one with a misdemeanor record, who was apparently not progressing despite the chances he had been given by the state.

Goodman looked over his bifocals at Derrick Smith, standing in the front of the crowded, loud 16th-floor courtroom at 100 Centre Street and gave the defendant his "hanging judge" face. He wanted this case disposed of and he wanted Smith to understand the serious position he was in.

"Mr. Smith, you have been offered a deal, I understand," he said, glancing over the sentencing memorandum. He looked up and stared at Derrick. "This is good for today only." It was past lunchtime and Goodman didn't want to delay this case any longer than he had to. He stressed the words "today only" so that Derrick would get the point.

"Your honor," Derrick said in a sad, distressed tone. "I'm 19 years old."

"Do I take it that you do not want to accept the plea offer?"

Derrick looked at me, then looked across the table at the assistant DA who hadn't even made eye contact with him, ever. The prosecutor was looking down at some papers in his briefcase preparing for the next deal in this assembly line of justice.

"Derrick," I said. "It's the best you're gonna get."

Derrick turned around and looked forlornly at his mother. "I can't do it," he said under his breath.

"It will be OK," she whispered back.

"It's terrible, just terrible," Derrick said.

"We'll set this for trial then, young man," Goodman said. "I'm looking at your record and I don't like what I see. Does the prosecution have anything?"

The young state's attorney stood up and, taking the hint from Goodman, asked that in light of the defendant's record, bail be revoked pending trial.

"I agree," Goodman said. "The defendant is hereby remanded to custody."

A city corrections officer came over as I was talking to Derrick.

"I'll be in touch," I said. I wasn't relishing this trial, since it was going to be a waste of everyone's time. A judge's time is valuable, at least the judge thinks so, and they don't like to have it wasted by someone demanding their right to trial. Most of the New York judges had been on the bench so long that they had forgotten about all of that innocent until proven guilty stuff.

The bailiff grabbed Derrick's arm and started to lead him away. Derrick turned, tears already forming in his eyes. "Mom," he wailed. "Mom, I can't do it."

She reached for him as he was pulled toward the holding pen and reassured him in her strongest possible voice that it was going to be okay, but I thought deep down she knew it wasn't.

I was gathering up his paperwork, clearing the table for the next attorney and hapless defendant, when I saw a commotion coming from the area to the right and behind Goodman's bench. It was in the area leading to the pens where they store the prisoners awaiting transport to Rikers.

Derrick's mother burst past the bar separating the spectators from the well of the courtroom followed by a couple of police officers and other court personnel who happened to have a better look at what was going on. I followed, but when I arrived it was too late. The bailiff was standing against the opposite wall from the window, the color had drained from his face to the extent that he looked like a black albino. He looked as if he was going to puke at any moment. Derrick Smith was nowhere in sight. Across from the bailiff, the window was broken and the cold October wind was blowing in.

"My baby," cried Ms. Smith. "That's my son!"

I looked out the window and forced myself to look down. Derrick had jumped out the window, fallen 16 stories, hit a corrections department bus and landed in the sallyport that the department used to load the buses for transport. Derrick had been decapitated and his body had split into three parts. There was blood everywhere.

Down below, witnesses who had been lunching calmly were recoiling with horror, some were sick and some were running, a few toward the scene, others away.

Up on the 16th floor, chaos ensued. Derrick's mother was hysterical, screaming and crying incoherently at her dead son, some 200 feet below her, lying in pieces on the dirty concrete. Judge Goodman was behind me, asking what the hell was going on, and the bailiff who had been in charge of Derrick was muttering to anyone who would listen that "he just tore himself away, there was nothing I could do." Inmates in the pen beyond the broken window were shouting like zoo animals excited by something beyond their cage and the guards unsnapped the covers to the Mace cans strapped to their utility belts. A few court officers tried to clear the hallway of gawkers.

Smith's mother had to be sedated and taken away by ambulance, leaving me to formally identify what was left of the young gang-banger. Standing in the sally port with the coroner's assistant and the investigation team, I flashed back briefly to Vietnam. Derrick looked remarkably like a grunt who had stepped on a booby-trapped 150-mm shell.

In the aftermath of Derrick's suicide, anti-drug law forces would try to make the young man a martyr, saying that the tough Rockefeller laws were responsible for the boy's suicide. The press used the event to point out government incompetence: the Court Administrator had requested that bars be placed on all windows the year before; the item had been budgeted, but then the request fell through the cracks and the work was never done.

During the course of my legal career I did represent some Italian defendants accused of having mob ties. One good friend of mine who I had the privilege of representing is an old-timer named Salvatore Aparo, a.k.a. Sammy Meatballs. He was accused of loansharking, racketeering, and whatever else the feds could throw at him. They alleged that he was an acting capo in the Genovese family. Sammy was 72 years old and in ill health when he was arrested on racketeering charges thanks to a bug worn by a young man he had sponsored in the family business. Heavy-set with thin lips and a full head of white hair, Sammy looks more like a Florida retiree than an acting capo in the Genovese crime family. He suffers from diabetes and has a bad heart.

Sammy's luck ran out thanks in part to a bookmaker's murder years before; ironically, it was a murder that Sammy had nothing to do with.

Tino Lombardi was a stand-up guy, friends recalled. A bookmaker with a large clientele, Tino was sitting in the San Guiseppi restaurant with an up-and-coming tough guy named Mike "Cookie" Durso when an unidentified gunman came in and shot the two men in late 1994. The killer was gunning for Tino, who died on the spot, but there was no reason to spare a witness and he fired on Durso as well. Durso reeled from a gunshot wound to the back of his head, bleeding profusely as other bystanders summoned help.

At first it didn't look like Durso was going to make it, but somehow the young goodfella managed to pull through. He had a big scar on his neck from the gunshots and surgery, but he wasn't disabled in the least. Sammy Meatballs took a liking to Durso. Sammy considered Mike as close, if not closer, than his own son.

The thirty-something Durso spent time in prison for a 1988 conviction on a $500,000 check fraud scheme, and had been around mobsters all of his life. On the surface, he was a loyal wiseguy, but beneath that layer Durso was seething. He knew, or at least he suspected, who had killed Tino and tried to kill him, and he wanted revenge. Nevertheless, killing is not something the Genovese family takes lightly and any vendetta would have to be approved by higher-ranking mobsters.

Durso pleaded his case to his superiors, and they declined his request for a hit on his attackers. The foundation for Durso's treachery had been laid. He began to feel he wasn't getting a decent return on the time and effort he was expending, but for another three years Durso remained a loyal soldier.

Then in 1998, Durso was arrested in connection with a Brooklyn murder and was facing serious jail time. He offered his services to the feds in exchange for leniency and started wearing a wire when he was around wiseguys. Gone are the days when confidential informants are required to tape a transmitter to their bodies and risk discovery and death. Mike Durso carried his bug in a ring or in a tiepin. For 500 hours, Durso recorded the intimate conversations of some of New York's toughest and most powerful mobsters.

The raids came in a pre-dawn invasion by law enforcement officers from the federal, state and local level who pounced on Sammy and 45 other wiseguys. It took 300 lawmen to bring them all in, and in typical FBI fashion, the leaders crowed about breaking "the Rolls Royce" of crime cartels.

In the end, faced with his own voice on tape bringing him down, Sammy Meatballs Aparo pleaded guilty in the spring of 2002 to racketeering and was sentenced to 70 months in prison. He did the time they gave him and now on federal probation for the rest of his life, he is an old man, sitting quietly in his small apartment. He may be a tough guy, but he is loyal to his family and friends and I think he is a great guy. I respect him very much and I am proud to call Sammy my friend.

CHAPTER 13

We all have an event in our lives that seems insignificant at first but that eventually changes who we are. I had one case that pushed my career in a direction that I never would have expected. Growing up around wiseguys I just expected that eventually I would become a criminal defense attorney to mobsters. I never thought that I would be one of those high-profile mob lawyers, but I did think that Italian mob cases would probably be my bread-and-butter. I could not have been more wrong.

At the time I was working the Lobster Shift at the Criminal Courts building because I was an insomniac. The Lobster Shift was an arraignment court that ran from 1 a.m. until 9 a.m. every day. In the 1980s when crack cocaine created an ongoing crime wave in New York City, the court system became so backlogged that it became necessary to run it 24 hours a day. Night Court went from 5 p.m. until 1 a.m. when the Lobster Shift began. The shift wasn't any different from what happened during the day, it was just that our day was the opposite of everyone else's.

It all started with a typical 18-b case. I was defending a young Asian kid who was accused of extorting money from restaurants on East Broadway and Eldridge Street in Chinatown. The kid was a member of some Chinese street gang — I forget which one, now. I needed an interpreter and I was introduced to a Taiwanese woman who was one of the toughest women I ever met. Let's call her Annie, although that's not her real name. She was somewhere between 30 and 50 and had once been a pool hustler. Her husband was still living in Taiwan where he operated a string of brothels.

It's sad to say that I don't even remember how that case turned out, but Annie apparently liked the way I handled it. Some time later she contacted me asking for help for a friend of hers who was accused of murder. Thanks to Annie, I would become one of the few westerners — lo fans — to infiltrate the very closed Chinese-American society that had been slowly building up in New York City. It is a world unto itself, something very few westerners will ever see.

Before the mid-1970s, there were perhaps 20,000 ethnic Chinese crammed into Manhattan's Chinatown, which made up a small six-block area surrounded by the Bowery and Mulberry Street on the east and west, and Canal and Worth streets to the north and south, respectively. Unlike their occidental counterparts, the Chinese were severely limited in the number of immigrants who would be let into the country. Up until 1965, racial quotas allowed just 105 Chinese to enter the U.S. each year.

However, after 1965, Chinese immigration exploded, and in just a few short years, more than 100,000 Chinese - mostly Cantonese - lived in Chinatown. This huge influx of immigrants changed the face of New York's Lower East Side once again. From the Irish and Germans who had settled the area in the 1840s, to the Jews and Italians who took over in the late 19th and early 20th Century, the Lower East Side between the Brooklyn Bridge and Houston Street was the place where refugees from Old World oppression became assimilated into the New World way of life. Now it was the Chinese who brought their ancient customs and traditions to the New World - including their own brand of organized crime.

Like their Jewish, Irish and Italian brethren, the Chinese mobsters trafficked in drugs, prostitution, shakedown rackets and the assorted vice that brings in ill-gotten gains. The gangs, or tongs, were clothed in respectability, with "merchants associations" and other fraternal groups often fronting for more sinister organizations. Older, more experienced gangsters used children - some as young as 12 or 13 to act as runners or strong-arm types (even a child with a weapon can be intimidating).

In New York City, the On Leong Tong controls the Chinese pastry business, which makes the moon cakes that are a traditional part of the famous Moon Festival. The On Leong Tong is a fraternal or business organization along the lines of the Elks or the Rotary to westerners. Chinese businessmen join the tong for the same reasons Americans do — to network and make friends. That part of the tong is not mysterious, malevolent or corrupt.

There is, of course, more to the story. The On Leong Tong is associated with a notorious street gang called the Ghost Shadows, of which there are several factions: the Mott Street Ghost Shadows, the Bayard Street faction and the Ghost Shadows which run Baxter and upper Mott Street past Canal.

For many years the dailo dai, or "Big big brother" of the On Leong Tong was Wing Young Chan, aka Big Head, a Chinese immigrant who had worked his way up through the ranks of the On Leong Tong from a dishwasher to head the On Leong Merchant's Association. Until he was taken down in a 1994 federal racketeering case, Chan held court at the popular 400-seat Harmony Palace on Mott Street, which was famous in Chinatown for the best dim sum and the most beautiful Chinese pop singers in New York City. He was suspected of ordering or taking part in several homicides of disloyal gang members and Chan had come to the attention of federal authorities for his role in the tong's drug and immigrant-smuggling schemes.

The On Leong Tong was divided up much the same way the Italian mobs were, with various factions, or families, further subdivided into crews. Street gangs are made up of members who follow their own dailo, the equivalent of an Italian capo. The dailo's power varies according to the gang he is affiliated with, how many members he controls and where he ranks with respect to the tong, or elder Chinese businessmen with Asian connections, both legal and illegal.

Chan's street dailos were Gumpie (Jian Lee) who ran the Mott Street Shadows, Robin and Robert Chee who controlled the very powerful and deadly Bayard faction and Crooked Tooth (Ah Cher), who ran the working houses.

The sailos, or little brothers, would use the Moon Festival as a chance to make money, selling a mooncake to a restaurant for $108. Why $108? Because that was "lucky money," the Chinese version of extortion. In lucky money the sum of the digits must equal 9.

Only the Ghost Shadows actually sell mooncakes. The other gangs in New York City's Chinatown — the Flying Dragons of Pell Street, the Tung On (Tsiung Tsing Tong), the Green Dragons of Elmhurst, Queens, the White Tigers of Flushing and the Brooklyn-based Gold Star would sell small orange tree plants for $108.

The payment of lucky money is an accepted and acceptable part of the Chinese culture. Even the businesses who are not being shaken down on a regular basis fully expect to have a sailo come in during Moon Festival to collect lucky money.

CHAPTER 14

Many of the young people who belonged to a street gang joined out of fear for their lives. Unaffiliated youngsters were often targeted by gang members and robbed, assaulted or otherwise intimidated. Joining a gang was seen as a way of self-preservation.

Leon was one such kid.

By the time I met him he was in his early 20s. He had been born in poverty in Hong Kong, the fourth son of a restaurant worker and a babysitter. His family had immigrated to the United States when he was a young child, whether legally or illegally I never found out. I did learn that Leon was never naturalized, which almost got him deported once.

When he was in junior high school he was approached by a street gang called the Ghost Shadows, but he rebuffed their attempts to lure him into their way of life. Rather than just move on to another recruit, the Ghost Shadows began to torment Leon. Eventually the Dailo, or "Big Brother" of a rival gang, the Flying Dragons, befriended Leon and initiated him as a member.

To be accepted as a member of the Flying Dragons Leon was required to commit five muggings without using any weapons while he was being watched by another member of the gang. Once he did this he was taken by the Flying Dragons to a small Buddhist temple on Pell Street in Chinatown where, along with three other proposed members, he drank the blood of a freshly killed chicken. Then he bowed three times before a statue of Buddha, before his Dailo, other gang members, and a leader of the Hip Sing Tong. Leon's first assignment with the Flying Dragons was to work as an armed guard at a Chinese restaurant that served as the front for a multimillion dollar gambling operation.

He had not forgotten the mistreatment he received from the Ghost Shadows. One night, along with some of his gang brothers, Leon cornered some Ghost Shadows outside a bar near Columbus Park in Chinatown. He put a gun to their heads and made them kneel down in the park by a bench and place their hands on the bench. Leon proceeded to use the butt of the gun to break every bone in their hands.

Eventually Leon became a Dailo himself and was operating several whorehouses in Philadelphia. He was arrested by federal agents for gun possession and trafficking in weapons. He received a light sentence but after his release from prison he was immediately detained by INS agents and sent to a deportation center in Louisiana. It was then that he learned that his mother had never bothered to get him naturalized.

Annie introduced me to Leon after he had been arrested for a vicious murder that occurred outside a Chinatown bar. He had been home just a few months and was hanging out with the Freemasons, a gang allied with the Flying Dragons. Most of Leon's associates in the Flying Dragons were away doing time so he began spending more and more time with the Freemasons, who operated a disco known as the Sinta Lounge. The Sinta was a sort-of DMZ in Chinatown where the various gangs could come and hang out. That didn't mean that altercations didn't occur there, of course.

Leon and some of the Freemasons were involved in a scuffle with members of the Vietnamese Born To Kill gang from Canal Street. The next morning the three BTK boys were found next to the bar, shot dead execution-style. Leon was among the six people the police brought in for questioning. Annie asked me to defend Leon, which I did. He was eventually cleared of any involvement in the murders. Three Freemasons were convicted of the slayings and are serving life terms.

Leon and I became very close during that time and eventually he came to work for me. Our relationship was more like brothers than employer/employee. Through Leon I met the Godfather of Chinatown, a man named Benny Ong, who was known as Uncle Benny or Uncle Seven. Benny was the head of the Hip Sing Tong and held court near Pell and Doyer streets in Chinatown, a place known as "The Bloody Angle" because of the number of people who were killed there. Arnold Rothstein once owned an opium den there.

As my business with Benny Eng and the Asian gangs increased, I eventually opened my office there, but I had to move out because it became a center of illegal activity for a Hip Sing Tong member. For example, one day I heard screaming on the staircase and watched as clients of mine kidnapped a man who owed them money for sneaking him into the country. There was also a nail salon where the girls would do more than polish your nails (they liked hanging out in my office). There was a clinic of doctors from China who practiced medicine without a license.

My mother and father took to Leon, as well. He would go with my family to Boston to visit my mother's family. Leon taught me the streets and alleys of Chinatown, of the Tongs and the snakeheads who smuggle human cargo into the United States.

Ah Gow was typical of the kind of clients I defended thanks to my work with Leon and Uncle Seven.

Zhang Ai Ping, a.k.a. "Ah Gow," was a typical member of a Chinese street gang. He pleaded guilty to a number of federal criminal charges in 2001, not the least of which included kidnapping, rape and armed robbery. His presentence report prepared for the U.S. Attorney's Office in New York reads like a one-man crime wave.

Ah Gow was born in Fuzhou in the Fujian Province of China on March 11, 1968, the fourth child of Li Mao Ying and Zhang Ho Hua. His parents are former teachers who still live in China. Along with a brother and sister, Ah Gow entered the United States illegally in 1992, with the help of a snakehead. He told the probation officer that he no longer had much contact with his family.

He was once treated for non-infectious tuberculosis, and told the probation officer that he has limited ability to read and write Chinese and speaks no English. His health remains poor from his bout with TB.

Faced with a $20,000 debt to the snakeheads for bringing him to America, with no opportunity to learn any kind of meaningful trade, the most money Ah Gow ever reported earning in a year was 1996, when he reported taxable income of $8,400. There was nowhere Ah Gow could turn, except to crime. Moreover, he took to his new career vigorously.

Ah Gow joined the Fukienese Flying Dragons, which the U.S. government considers an on-going criminal enterprise. He first came to the attention of the government in 1994, when with three other men, Ah Gow robbed a Forsythe Street apartment where approximately 20 people had gathered. It was payday for the workers at a Chinatown restaurant, and the men knew there would be significant cash at the apartment. When one of the workers tried to hide a small amount of his hard-earned wage, Ah Gow beat the man severely. The Flying Dragons escaped with approximately $1,200.

The same month, Ah Gow, Huang Yong and two other men robbed a mah jongg parlor near Confucius Plaza in Chinatown, again beating one of their victims. The gangsters this fled with more than $12,000 and some jewelry and guns. Later in the summer, Ah Gow and a street brother staged a "robbery" of a delivery truck. The driver had tipped them to the contents of the truck and Ah Gow stole $6,000.

They later robbed a gambling den run by the rival Tung On gang on Division Street, where they received $40,000. At the same time, the government charged, they were extorting money from a Chinese dentist in Chinatown. Returning to the restaurant-payday MO, Ah Gow stole immigration documents and between $5,000 and $6,000 from an apartment in New Jersey.

In the fall of 1994, Ah Gow's dailo, Lin Bo, kidnapped a group of five illegal aliens, and had Ah Gow hold them at gunpoint for several days. The aliens were being held until their snakehead paid a $20,000 ransom. For his part in the scam, Ah Gow received $1,000.

When he reported to prison to begin serving his 135-month sentence - which would include English as a Second Language and vocational training - Ah Gow left a wife and six-year-old son behind in Brooklyn.

When the time came for Ah Gow to enter his plea, he was embittered and angry with America and the government, which he thought, was persecuting him. After all, he reasoned, the girl he was accused of raping - one of the illegal aliens he was guarding - hadn't protested that much when he lay on top of her. She had it coming, he felt, and that shouldn't have been considered a crime. Once Ah Gow finishes his sentence, assuming he's still alive, he can expect to be deported.

CHAPTER 15

Leon instructed me in the ways of the gambling dens and Chicken houses (whorehouses to lo fans like you and me) and which streets belonged to which gangs. Thanks to Leon I became nationally known as an Asian gang expert. I have been cited in magazines, newspaper articles and even in textbooks.

Leon taught me how to collect from Oriental clients, too. This is a typical collection night for me:

Flushing, Queens 12:30 a.m. It was dark and raining and I was driving through the back streets of this neighborhood that looks like a collision between a war zone and a strip mall in Seoul. I was wearing camo fatigues, an MIA ballcap and I had a baseball bat across my lap as I steered my beat-up Toyota Corolla/mobile office looking for a spot to park. Turned from a piece of hardened pine, the bat has never been used on a ball diamond; instead, it serves as a persuader for reticent customers. I refer to the bat as "Fate." When a client is slow to pay, I wave the bat back and forth, warning the client that he is tempting fate.

5

I recently did some legal work for a Korean guy who runs a couple of working houses and the guy wouldn't come through. Not only did I manage to get Mr. Park's girls out on bail, I managed to keep them from going straight from Rikers Island to INS detention, but Mr. Park doesn't think that's worth paying for.

Bargaining with a Korean pimp is tricky. You have to know when to negotiate and when to threaten. With Mr. Park, the proprietor of a massage parlor above a dim sum parlor near the edge of Flushing, the time for negotiation had passed. That's why that night I brought Fate with me.

Taking the steps two at a time in a burst of adrenaline, I called out to my client.

"Park!" I shouted, the word sounding more like a pit-bull's bark than English. "Park, you yellow sonuvabitch!"

I pushed my way into the lobby of Park's working house. As it is just a little past prime time, this house busy; there were two Chinese men waiting, reading Chinese newspapers. They looked at me with wide eyes. I must have seemed like a crazy man to them, a lo-fan in battle fatigues with a bat, screaming as he ran up the stairs.

Park came quickly from a back room and motioned me to come with him, never saying a word. He was clearly angry at me for causing such a commotion in the house, but I didn't care. As we walked to the back, girls' heads popped out through curtains which block access to the many alcoves and rooms in the labyrinthine flat.

Once inside Park's office, I immediately crossed over to the smaller Korean man.

"I asked you nicely to pay me and you promised to pay me. I'm not asking any more."

To punctuate my assertion, I snapped my wrist like a pitcher throwing a high inside curve and Fate crashed into a lamp on Park's desk. The light bulb exploded and the shade collapsed as the lamp falls to the floor.

"You owe me $1,000 for the work I did for you. I know you have it…"

The door burst open and a young Korean man, well dressed, with slicked back hair and glasses so shiny it is hard to see his eyes, bounded into the room. He was carrying a .22-caliber pistol, an automatic, in his hand. The safety was off.

"What's going on?" the young man asked.

Park, regaining his courage now that his ally was in the room, spoke for the first time.

"Frank here thinks we owe him some money," Park said. "He's acting tough."

"Oh, a tough guy, huh?" the Korean hood says, almost to himself. "I'm a tough guy, too." He made the mistake of waving the pistol around.

I backed the punk into the wall and grabbed the hand holding the weapon, wrenching it out of his hand. Park apparently didn't like that.

"Frank!" Park yells. "Frank, all right! I'll pay."

"Here's $750. I need to keep some cash here," he says, handing the wad to Frank. "I'll get you the rest. Just get out of here now."

I tossed the gun behind the couch.

Business is business. The next time Park runs into trouble with the law, he knows who to call. He'll call me and I will bail his ass out and the whole routine will happen again.

Some collections are easy, others less so. Earlier in the week I visited a Korean mama-san to collect money, and that time I had not been forced to use any strong-arm tactics. The mama-sans are not necessarily easier to collect from; sometimes I have to get rough, but that night, Madam Mink had been easy to persuade.

She owed me from a late-night call I received a few months before. The telephone's jangling jolted me from another Vietnam nightmare, and it took me a few minutes to figure out what continent I was on. The screaming voice on the other end of the phone didn't help orient me at all.

"Frankie, bali…bali!" came the voice through the receiver. It was a working girl telling me to hurry. It took me a couple of minutes to get the story straight. A raid had shut down Madam Mink's Astoria, Queens working house and three of her best girls were in stir downtown. She wanted me down there immediately to get them out.

I moved as fast as I could and by 7:30 the next morning, the girls were ROR'd from the precinct lock-up. The desk sergeant was a fellow vet and gave me a break.

In front of the stationhouse, the girls fussed over me and blew me kisses, telling me to come visit them soon.

Later, it was time to collect from Madam Mink.

"Frankie, you come see me!" the heavy-set Mama-san said as I puffed my way up the stairs.

"Mama-san, how are you," I said, trying to be nice. "How come you don't return my phone calls?"

"I'm very busy, Frankie," she said. "Very busy place here."

"I can see that," I said.

I looked around and surveyed the ornate sitting area where a couple of girls lounged around, looking bored. There wasn't a customer in the place, but it was early. This mama-san probably pulled in a cool ten grand each week, almost all of that profit. She paid off the local dailo, the girls, and probably a cop or immigration officer or two.

"Mama-san, I'm here for my money."

"Money? What money?" The mama-san adopted the Koreans' favorite ploy whenever westerners started talking about money: "I don't understand what you are saying."

"C'mon," I said. "For the call you made the other night. Remember the raid? You owe me $600, for that plus the court appearance later."

"I give you $300," she countered.

"No. I need $600," I said.

"You take a girl," mama-san said, waving her hand toward the bored young ladies in the sitting room.

"Mama-san, the girls are very nice. They are very pretty and they do a nice job. But they can't feed my daughter."

"Four hundred."

"Mama-san, six hundred. That's what we agreed to."

"You come back Monday," Mink said, playing dumb. "The girls work this weekend and I have your money."

I lost my temper. The girls had called me 15 times the night they were arrested, begging and pleading for me to get them out. The stupid whores were even busted by the same cop who got them two weeks earlier. They never look at the guy's face.

"You fucking pig!" I shouted, slamming his hand against the doorway. "I got you out of a $1,000 fine and community service! They were going to shut down your fucking gook shop and I pulled your ass out of the fucking fire. I'll slit your fucking throat, you don't pay me six fucking hundred dollars right fucking now!"

The mama-san never batted an eye. Words that would have started a race riot and sexual harassment lawsuit in a better section of town didn't phase her. She stared at me, weighing her options. Negotiate, play dumb, pay up.

"Ok. Ok. Come with me," Mink relented and waved me into a small office behind a beaded curtain. She left me standing there for a moment and soon returned with a lock box. Reaching inside her muumuu, she pulled a key from between her breasts and unlocked the box. Inside were several stacks of bills: twenties, fifties and hundreds. Nothing smaller. She grabbed the stack of hundreds and counted off six Franklins. When she noticed me looking at the box, she shut it quickly and locked it.

"This is the small one," she said, somewhat proudly.

"Then why the fuck did you give me such a hard time?" I asked.

"It's my money. I earned it."

"I think they earned some of it," I said, referring to the working girls.

"I take the risk," mama-san said. "I earn the money."

While it's never pleasant having to collect my fees that way, Leon taught me that Asians do business differently than Westerners. I never would have made it in this kind of work without him. The language that I have to use may be offensive to us, but for Asians it's not.

CHAPTER 16

I'll never forget the day that I lost Leon. It was one of the worst days of my life and I wouldn't wish that feeling of loss on my worst enemy. I was uptown in a diner waiting for my bookie. I had a terrible hangover. My pager went off and I recognized the number as belonging to the head of NYPD's Asian Gang Squad. Obviously our paths had crossed many times before.

"What the hell do you want, paging me at 7:30 in the morning?" I growled.

"I need you down here on Catherine Street near Madison to ID a body," the detective said.

I told him that I didn't do that kind of thing.

"Frank," he said, gently. "It's Leon."

His words hit me like a shot to the stomach and I began to get the feelings I got when I was about to experience flashbacks. I swallowed a handful of tranquilizers as I fought my way through morning traffic.

At Catherine Street I saw a body bag on the ground by a telephone booth. The detective opened the bag and I saw that it was Leon. His pager was still on and it read 4444444. In Chinese four sounds like death.

The detective asked if I knew anything about this. I just stared at him. I knew this was payback from some rival gang; I also think it was a subtle message to me. I said nothing to the detective and I have nothing more to say about Leon's death. I had lost my Chinese brother.

After Leon's death I managed to press on with my career as a street lawyer, but eventually I began to feel burned out. I remember the day I finally crossed the line and knew I had to get out of that kind of work.

I had just walked into 100 Centre Street when I bumped into a guy who had been working there as a bailiff as long as I could remember. I had not seen him in some time, and we greeted each other like the old friends we were.

"Frank, I'm so glad I ran into you," he said, a big smile on his face. "I'm getting out of this place!"

"What do you mean?" I asked.

"I'm retiring! The wife and I have a condo in Tampa and next week we're moving down there for good. Thirty years in this hell-hole is enough."

I congratulated him on his luck and started walking toward the holding cells where I was to meet a client. My mind kept going back to my friend and how I would never be able to retire if I kept going the way I was going now. There was just not enough money in being a street lawyer. I saw myself as an old man, dragging my ass to court day after day until I just dropped dead.

As I got closer to the cells, I started to sweat and I had trouble breathing. I thought I was having a heart attack, but it was just stress. My feet started to feel like they weighed 100 pounds each and it was hard to walk. I began to get angry and it looked to me like the men in those cells were not people, but animals. I felt hopeless.

I managed to get through the hearing but I knew I could not go back again. I had to find something else to do. It was then that I learned just how much worth society placed on me.

I tried to get a job with the New York City School System, which was desperate for teachers. They didn't want me, even though I was a veteran and a lawyer. The fact that I had taught school in Korea didn't seem to matter.

Over the next few months I tried everything I could to get another job without success. One place even told me I was too old. I didn't have the energy to file a discrimination claim. Eventually I got a job as a server in for a coffee chain. There I was, in my 50s, with a law degree and a veteran, wearing an apron making lattes.

Eventually I managed to go back to one of the only places I felt at home -- the Coast Guard. I got transferred from the reserves to active duty. The first day I put on my uniform, my hands were shaking. I didn't want to wear the service ribbons I had earned, but a friend talked me into it, telling me I should do so in honor of all of my brothers who never came home from Vietnam.

I suffer from Post-Traumatic Stress Disorder from my service in Nam and 9-11. On that September day I was serving in the Coast Guard Reserves and was called up immediately under Title 10, Presidential Orders. It goes without saying how devastating that time was for all of us. I was in public affairs and spent much of my time at Ground Zero because I was a military escort for the media. I wrote news releases and articles, and was a participant in media interviews.

From the Coast Guard Station near Battery Park, just a mortar shot away from what everyone now called Ground Zero, I was pressed into patrol duty on a forty-foot craft. This was no weekend drill, this was war.

As I stood guard that night on deck, watching the surreal glow of the smoke-filled sky over what was once the center of the world financial market, the irony of the situation was not lost on me. I watched the 270-foot cutter Tahoma slip into the harbor, armed with her 50-caliber guns and 76mm cannon, and I thought back to a promise an oracle in the shape of a chief petty officer made to me long ago.

"Sure, you'll be patrolling off Coney Island," the CPO said to me. "The Coast Guard's the place for you."

Thirty years late, but "Merv" had kept his word.

Leon was gone, but I knew he would want me to go on. I continued working on Asian cases, but more and more I found myself returning to my own roots, the world of my father and grandfather. That world has changed immeasurably since they were active on the streets. The government has enacted laws that have curtailed the activities of the Italian mobs, and the changing culture of the borgatas has done just as much to end that way of life. The unity of purpose has been replaced by a dog-eat-dog philosophy. The old-timers just sit by and wonder what happened to that thing of theirs.

"We're the end of the totem pole," one of them once said to me.

In a way that is a good thing. The children of mobsters are moving on and finding their own way in the world. While they embrace their culture and heritage, they realize that there is more to life than bookmaking, loansharking, and shaping up.

Take, for example, the late Anthony (Tony West) DeLutro, an alleged member of the Carlo Gambino family, and his son, John, whom we like to call "Baby John." My father loved Tony West and he used to take me to the Ravenite Social Club on Mulberry Street. In those days social clubs were a familiar sight in Italian neighborhoods. This was before FBI surveillance.

Tony West helped me when I was a singer by getting me bookings in nightclubs and he brought me around to meet people in the record business. He was a great guy and only wanted to help me.

Baby John DeLutro is like a cousin to me. As a young man he started a cafe in his mother's dress shop. He worked long and hard hours and has become a real American success story. He started out stuffing homemade cannoli shells with the best ricotta and sugar recipe imaginable and serving the pastry with espresso or cappucino. As the years went by he expanded the cafe by adding other pastries and delicacies. Today, my great friend Baby John DeLutro is known as the "Cannoli King of Little Italy." Considering how many vendors sell those pastries, that is quite an accomplishment. To find Baby John's place just look for the tour buses and the crowds. No visit to Little Italy is complete without a visit to Baby John's Caffe Palermo.

Looking back on my life, there are some things that I would change, as we probably all would. But for the most part I don't regret much. To go from a punk kid named Frankie 13 to an attorney representing the people society has forgotten, protecting their rights and fighting for their freedom seems like some kind of bad novel. Some of the things that have happened to me might seem unbelievable, but everything I've written here is documented.

My family became part of the fabric of America under the shadow of the Williamsburg Bridge and that bridge has always held a special place in my heart. The Williamsburg Bridge of my father and grandfather is gone, though, and I find that rather tragic. Recently with my friend Robert Mirenda and I spent some time taking some photographs on what is left of Willett Street by Delancy on the Lower East Side. Projects replaced the tenements where my father grew up.

I walked under the Williamsburg Bridge, with all of its new construction. But in my imagination I could hear the sounds of my father's generation — the stickball playing, the sounds of street cart vendors, the horseshit battles and gang fights, the name calling.

It's a time that is gone but for those who know and listen carefully, those boys are still playing, fighting and plotting schemes.

You can almost see their shadows under the Williamsburg Bridge.

POSTSCRIPT

BROOKLYN FEDERAL CORRECTIONAL FACILITY
by Frank Bari

— I shake inside, as the Corrections Officer remembers me and thanks
  me for helping him out years ago- with his VA claim—
— I look at the faceless rows of inmates being visited by family — I
  remember this as a part of life—
— I don't know what has happened to me— since I was a top Lawyer
  here—
— My Father's died— I've lost any monies I had — I'm getting older
  now and I'm afraid of the cancer and diabetes that's in me -sticking
  me like punji sticks—
— I swallow 14 pills a day and inject two shots of insulin in my
  stomach—
— At night I booby trap my bed and my wife falls over the trip
  wire—
— I dream of people I loved who are gone—
— I see the trees and smiling faces of Vietnamese with their rusted
  teeth sticking out—-
— I feel the welcome cool breeze-that used to come magically through
  the Mekong Delta in the evenings—
— the air smelling of burned shit and Nuoc Mom

— my client comes —in a wheelchair into the Attorney booth—
— his hip was shot half off in a drug fight— he takes more psychotic drugs then I— Haldol, Prozac, Thorizine, Stelizine and so on—
— we talk of his case— my adrenaline runs — as I'm in combat— I can attack Prosecutors from their right and left Flanks—Their FNG's— I have to save my client's life—after 9/11/01— the rain and hail hits the wood boards that make my roof—
— I jump the thump -thump-thump— as the bodies splashed in front of me at the
— Twin Tower attack— covering my Coast Guard Blue Uniform in Red—
— "Old Andy", who boarded junks and sampans with me on the brown rivers of Vietnam always comes to mind— he killed himself in 1993 —all dressed in his Mekong Bandanna—\he placed a .38 in his mouth -and was gone—he had my photo with him and his Mother buried him with it—
— I have to concentrate on my war now and save my clients ————
— My good Friend Francisco, always writes me, "WELCOME HOME."
— But I don't think I will ever be home again— WRITTEN FROM THE BOWELS OF BROOKLYN'S PRISON—
I am still at WAR! —-